Multilingual Biomedical Text Processing (MultilingualBIO 2020)

Marseille, France
11 – 16 May 2020

Editor:

Maite Melero

ISBN: 978-1-7138-1270-8

Printed from e-media with permission by:

Curran Associates, Inc.
57 Morehouse Lane
Red Hook, NY 12571

Some format issues inherent in the e-media version may also appear in this print version.

Association for Computational Linguistics
209 N. Eighth Street
Stroudsburg, Pennsylvania 18360

Phone: 1-570-476-8006
Fax: 1-570-476-0860

acl@aclweb.org

Additional copies of this publication are available from:

Curran Associates, Inc.
57 Morehouse Lane
Red Hook, NY 12571 USA
Phone: 845-758-0400
Fax: 845-758-2633
Email: curran@proceedings.com
Web: www.proceedings.com

LREC 2020 Workshop
Language Resources and Evaluation Conference
11-16 May 2020

Multilingual Biomedical Text Processing (MultiligualBIO 2020)

PROCEEDINGS

Editor:
Maite Melero, Barcelona Supercomputing Center (Spain)

Proceedings of the LREC 2020 Workshop on Multilingual Biomedical Text Processing (MultiligualBIO 2020)

Edited by: Maite Melero, Barcelona Supercomputing Center (Spain)

For more information:
European Language Resources Association (ELRA)
9 rue des Cordelières
75013, Paris
France
http://www.elra.info
Email: lrec@elda.org

Introduction

Welcome to MultilingualBIO 2020, the LREC2020 Workshop on "Multilingual Biomedical Text Processing" . As the COVID-19 pandemic unrolls during the first months of 2020 around the world, the need for strong AI and NLP technologies for biomedical text is more evident than ever. As in other NLP areas, we are currently witnessing fast developments, with improved access, analysis and integration of healthcare-relevant information from heterogeneous content types, including electronic health records, medical literature, clinical trials, medical agency reports or patient-reported information available form social media and forums. There is an increasing automation of tasks in many critical areas, such as detecting interactions or supporting clinical decision. However, progress is very uneven depending on the language. Main achievements in processing biomedical text are almost restricted to English, with most other languages lagging behind in this respect, due to lack of annotated resources, incomplete vocabularies and insufficient in-domain corpora. More effort from the research community is needed to endow these languages with the necessary resources. The second edition of MultilingualBIO, at the LREC 2020 Conference, aims at promoting the development of biomedical text processing resources and components in languages beyond English, exploring the use of novel methodological advances for a diversity of tasks in the domain.

Organizers:

Maite Melero, Barcelona Supercomputing Center (Spain)
Martin Krallinger, Barcelona Supercomputing Center (Spain)
Aitor Gonzalez-Agirre, Barcelona Supercomputing Center (Spain)
Marta Villegas, Barcelona Supercomputing Center (Spain)
Jordi Armengol-Estapé, Barcelona Supercomputing Center (Spain)

Program Committee:

Casimiro Carrino, Barcelona Supercomputing Center (Spain)
Nigel Collier, University of Cambridge (UK)
Marta R. Costa-Jussà, Universitat Politècnica de Catalunya (Spain)
Hercules Dalianis, Stockholm University (Sweden)
Cristina España-Bonet, DFKI (Germany)
Jin-Dong Kim, DBCLS / ROIS (Japan)
Patrik Lambert, ICONIC (Ireland)
Anália Lourenço, Universidad de Vigo (Spain)
Paloma Martínez, Universidad Carlos III (Spain)
Raquel Martínez Unanue, UNED (Spain)
Roser Morante, Vrije Universiteit Amsterdam (Holland)
Patrick Ruch, University of Applied Sciences (Switzerland)
Isabel Segura-Bedmar, Universidad Carlos III (Spain)
Pierre Zweigenbaum, CNRS (France)

Table of Contents

Proceedings of MultilingualBIO 2020, pages 1–8
Language Resources and Evaluation Conference (LREC 2020), Marseille, 11–16 May 2020

Detecting Adverse Drug Events from Swedish Electronic Health Records Using Text Mining

Maria Bampa, Hercules Dalianis
Department of Computer and System Science
Stockholm University
{maria.bampa, hercules}@dsv.su.se

Abstract

Electronic Health Records are a valuable source of patient information which can be leveraged to detect Adverse Drug Events (ADEs) and aid post-mark drug-surveillance. The overall aim of this study is to scrutinize text written by clinicians in Swedish Electronic Health Records (EHR) and build a model for ADE detection that produces medically relevant predictions. Natural Language Processing techniques are exploited to create important predictors and incorporate them into the learning process. The study focuses on the five most frequent ADE cases found in the electronic patient record corpus. The results indicate that considering textual features, can improve the classification performance by 15% in some ADE cases, compared to a method that used structured features. Additionally, variable patient history lengths are included in the models, demonstrating the importance of the above decision rather than using an arbitrary number for a history length. The experimental findings suggest the importance of the variable window sizes as well as the importance of incorporating clinical text in the learning process, as it is highly informative towards ADE prediction and can provide clinically relevant results.

1. Introduction

With the introduction of Electronic Health Records (EHRs) an abundant of information has become available. This provides unique opportunities not only for monitoring patients but also for the use of these data sources in secondary research. An EHR contains all the key information regarding a patient case over time, including demographics, medication, diagnoses and procedures, vital signs, laboratory results and hand-written text. Some of the aforementioned are captured in a structured format, for example, drug and diagnoses codes are represented in the ATC and ICD-10 format respectively. However, the vast majority of this information is captured in an unstructured and non-standardized format, i.e. clinical free text notes.

As EHRs are a vast source of patient medical history, they have enabled more efficient retrospective research in various domains, namely epidemiology, public health research, outcome research and drug surveillance (Weiskopf et al., 2013). Specifically, in drug surveillance, EHRs are an alternative method to evaluate drug risk and mitigate the problem of Adverse Drug Reactions (ADEs). ADEs refer to injuries caused by medication errors, allergic reactions or overdoses, and are related to drugs[1]. They can happen in different settings of patient care, from hospitals to outpatient settings, after a drug has been released to the market. In the United States alone, each year, they account for approximately 2 million hospital stays, more than 1 million emergency department visits and cause prolonged hospitalizations[2]. Due to several factors and barriers that come with ADE reporting, they are heavily under-reported in EHRs, causing in that way a long-term burden in the healthcare sector and in the individuals suffering an ADE. Nevertheless, it is estimated that about half of the ADEs are preventable[3], indicating the importance of directing research in post-market drug surveillance, to reduce withdrawal of drugs from the market and more importantly lessen human suffering.

EHRs are representative for a wide range of patients, specifically for patients with different diseases, in different age and gender distribution. Data and text mining methods can be employed to leverage this information and predict unwanted ADEs. In the side of structured data sources stemming from EHRs, previous research has mainly focused on utilizing specific predictors, for example ICD-10[4], ATC[5] or laboratory results, to predict ADEs. A recent work by Bamba and Papapetrou (2019) has utilized the temporal and hierarchical aspect of the previously mentioned data sources to predict ADEs and concluded in a framework with high classification performance. Additionally, they experimented with variable history lengths before the occurrence of an ADE and indicated its importance in the experiments. However, they only utilized features in a structured format and did not consider important information that can be found in the text that accompanies the majority of patients.

To meet the challenges posed by narrative data, text mining is commonly used to extract and retrieve relevant information by recognizing statistical patterns in the text. In previous research the use of Natural Language Processing (NLP) has been investigated for obtaining models that are able to predict unseen ADEs from EHRs. For example, Eriksson et al. (2013) constructed a dictionary from a Danish EHR and managed to identify 35,477 unique possible ADEs. Henriksson et al. (2015) have modeled Swedish EHR data in ensembles of semantic spaces and reported

[1] ADE, `https://health.gov/hcq/ade.asp`

[2] https://health.gov/our-work/health-care-quality/adverse-drug-events

[3] https://psnet.ahrq.gov/primer/medication-errors-and-adverse-drug-events

[4] ICD-10, `https://www.icd10data.com`

[5] ATC, `https://www.whocc.no/atc_ddd_index/`

improved performance in 27 datasets. Additionally, An NLP system named MedLEE, was used to create discharge summaries and outperformed traditional and previous automated adverse event detection methods (Melton and Hripcsak, 2005).

To the best of our knowledge existing data mining approaches for ADE prediction in Swedish EHRs, have been mainly focusing on utilizing specific structured data types. Moreover, many of the studies do not take into account the importance of considering variable window lengths depending on the ADE studied. Exploiting a very large patient history window length can add noise to the data and a very small window size can eliminate useful and informative predictors.

Contributions. This paper, follows the work of Bamba and Papapetrou (2019) utilizing variable window lengths, but instead incorporating in the machine learning process textual features, rather than structured, that can be highly informative predictors for the specific ADEs studied. Specifically, the state-of-the-art is extended by:

1. including textual features, using the n-gram model and tf*idf weighting,
2. exploring variable patient history trajectories for each of the ADEs
3. benchmarking the proposed approach in three classification models.

As shown in Section 5 the incorporation of text features in the learning process, combined with the different window lengths for each ADE can provide improvements in the classification performance while providing medical sound predictions.

2. Related Work

EHRs contain a wealth of longitudinal patient history which can be leveraged to create models for personalized-care and provide clinically relevant insights. Post-market drug surveillance based on EHRs can lead to further investigation and regulatory warnings about drugs (Karimi et al., 2015) and a decrease in drug withdrawal from the market. However, EHRs suffer from several disadvantages such as under-reporting, absence of protocols and reporting bias (Karimi et al., 2015), and in that way, the prevalence of an ADE cannot be estimated with full confidence. Previous research on EHRs tried to tackle problems like the aforementioned, utilizing a wide range of predictors to identify ADEs. This section summarizes research conducted towards ADE prediction from EHRs. The first paragraph presents research that utilized the structured data founds in EHRs; the rest of this section describes works that have focused on exploiting the textual features of EHRs to predict ADEs.

Studies that use structured clinical codes (diagnoses and/or drug codes) focus on different ways of representing them by internationally defined standards (ICD diagnosis and ATC drug codes respectively) and conclude that predictive performance was significantly improved when using the concept of hierarchies (Zhao et al., 2014; Zhao et al., 2015b). Other related work utilizes clinical codes and clinical measurements while taking their temporal aspect into account, for identifying ADEs (Zhao et al., 2015c). Studies in this area typically exploit logistic regression (Harpaz et al., 2010) or Random Forests (Zhao et al., 2015a) applied in clinical codes to identify ADEs. Using only laboratory abnormalities Park et al. (2011) used the underlying temporality of these events to predict ADEs. Finally, (Bagattini et al., 2019) focused on lab results extracted from EHRs and proposed a framework that transforms sparse and multivariate time series to single valued presentations that can be used be any classifier to identify ADEs; they conclude that taking into account the sparsity of the feature space can positively affect the predictive performance and be effectively utilized to predict ADEs.

The unstructured sections of EHRs, i.e. free-text, have also been used to detect ADEs. The main approach in this line of research is to employ NLP techniques to transform the text in some form of structured features in order to feed machine learning classifiers (Karimi et al., 2015). For example, (Wang et al., 2009) and (Melton and Hripcsak, 2005) have both used the MedLee NLP system to identify adverse drug event signals and they outperformed traditional and previous automated adverse event detection methods. MedLee is a natural language processor that extracts information from text employing a vocabulary and grammar and has been extended to cover a spectrum of applications (Melton and Hripcsak, 2005). LePendu et al. (2013) proposed a method to annotate the clinical notes found in EHRs and using medical terminologies, transformed them to a de-identified matrix. Eriksson et al. (2013) identified a wide range of drugs by creating an ADE dictionary from a Danish EHR. Furthermore, Henriksson et al. (2015) focused on Swedish EHR data and reported improvement in ADE detection by exploiting multiple semantic spaces built on different sizes, as opposed to a single semantic space. Finally, the combination of local and global representation of words and entities has proven to yield better accuracy than using them in isolation for ADE prediction according to Henriksson (2015).

3. Data

The clinical dataset Stockholm EPR Structured and Unstructured ADE corpus, (SU-ADE Corpus)[6] used in this study consists of information representing more than a million patients from Karolinska University Hospital in Sweden. The SU-ADE Corpus is an extract from the research infrastructure Health Bank (the Swedish Health Record Research Bank) at DSV/Stockholm University that contain patients from 512 clinical units encompassing the years 2007-2014 originally from the TakeCare CGM electronic patient record system at Karolinska University Hospital (Dalianis et al., 2015).

[6]Ethical approval was granted by the Stockholm Regional Ethical Review Board under permission no. 2012/834-31/5.

Both structured and unstructured data are part of the database and are also timestamped. Structured data are labelled using common encoding systems such as the Anatomical Therapeutic Chemical Classification System (ATC) for medications, the International Statistical Classification of Diseases and Related Health Problems, 10th Edition (ICD-10) for diagnoses as well as the Nomenclature, Properties and Units (NPU) coding system[7] for clinical laboratory measurements. Regarding unstructured format, each patient is described by a text that is written in free format by clinicians; the SU-ADE Corpus contains more than 500 million tokens, in total.

The ADE groups of this study were selected as they are some of the most frequent in the SU-ADE Corpus. The specific 5 ADE cases were chosen for comparison reasons to the paper by Bamba and Papapetrou (2019)(see section 5). The experiments are formulated as a binary classification task; according to patients' ICD-10 codes, labels are assigned to each of them. More concretely, each patient in a dataset is described by a class label that denotes if that patient has an ADE or not. Negative examples are denoted as 0, while positive examples are denoted as 1. The following procedure was adopted: Patients that are assigned a specific ADE code are considered positive to that ADE (Stausberg and Hasford, 2011), while patients that are not assigned that specific ADE code but have been given a code that belongs to the same disease taxonomy are considered ADE negative. For example, patients that are given the ADE code D61.1 (drug induced aplastic anaemia) are positive to that specific ADE, on the other side, patients that are given codes that belong to D61.x with x $\neq$ 0 are considered ADE negative. A list and an explanation for each dataset can be seen in Table 1.

The ICD-10 codes serve only as reference for the extraction of the sub-datasets and the subsequent class labeling. In that way, from the original corpus we extract all the patients that have at least one reference of the following codes in their history: D61.*, E27.*, G62.*, L27.*,T80.* (* denotes every possible digit from one to nine). Following that, we create the sub-datasets according to the ADE codes and assign the class labels as described above. The patients are then described by text written by a healthcare expert. The main methodology is described in section 4.

4. Methods

The following section provides a description of the methods used in this work. In Figure 1 the process of the method that was used is depicted.

4.1. Text Preprocessing

Following the class labeling, text assigned to each patient is then pre-processed, so as to bring it in a format that is analyzable and predictable. Swedish is different from English thus the techniques used are different, for example

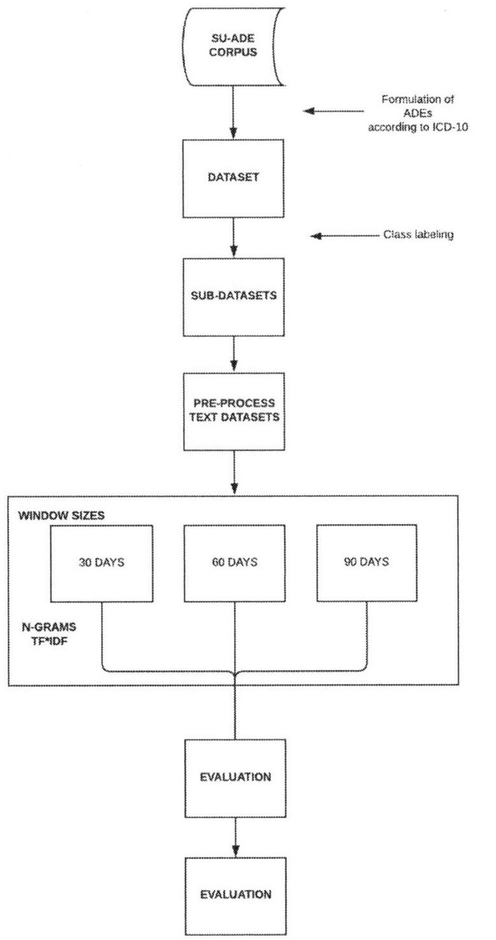

Figure 1: Depiction of the method flow. Starting from the SU-ADE corpus to the creation of the 5 ADE datasets and finally evaluation of the model.

Swedish is a highly inflected language as well as a compounding language, similar to German.

Since the datasets that are handled in this work are very large, to help with the consistency of the expected output, all the words were lower-cased. Also, noise and Swedish stop word removal was carried out to help reduce the number of features before classification and produce consistent results. Stop-words do not convey any significant semantics in the output result, consequently they were discarded. Finally, lemmatisation was performed to transform the Swedish words into their dictionary form, a procedure highly important in our study as the Swedish language is highly inflectional (Carlberger et al., 2001). The library used for stop word removal and lemmatisation was NLTK[8].

[7] NPU, `http://www.ifcc.org/ifcc-scientific-division/sd-committees/c-npu/`

[8] Natural Language Toolkit, `https://www.nltk.org/`

Dataset	Description	Positive	Negative
D61.*	Aplastic Anaemia	557 (D61.1)	94($D61.x$)
E27.*	Adrenocortical insufficiency	55($E27.3$)	219 (E27.x)
G62.*	Polyneuropathy	79($G62.0$)	672 (G62.x)
L27.*	Generalized skin eruption	391 (L27.0)	172 (L27.x)
T80.*	Infusion complications	502 (T80.8)	135 (T80.x)

Table 1: The 5 most common ADE cases studied. The * under the Dataset column: denotes every possible code under the specific category included in the dataset; column *Positive* depicts the number of ADE positive patients and the specific ADE code is in parentheses; column *Negative* depicts the number of ADE negative patients where x is any number besides the last digit of the ADE depicted in each row and the examples are in parentheses.

4.2. Window Sizes

Furthermore, as this study focuses on events that occur over various time periods, the sub-datasets are created on different window sizes, in order to investigate potentially informative patient trajectories for specific ADEs. 30, 60 and 90 days window sizes are investigated. In those cases, the day when the ADE was registered was excluded from the learning process, as we are interested in predicting patients with a potential ADE.

4.3. Word Vectors

The following representations of the text at word level are considered: *unigrams, bigrams, trigrams (n-grams)* and *tf*idf* (in a uni-gram word level) where *tf* stands for term frequency and *idf* for inverse document frequency (Van Rijsbergen, 1979).

The n-gram model predicts the occurrence of the n-th word based on the occurrence of n-1 words in the document. This follows the Markov assumption that only the previous words affect the next word (Manning et al., 1999). For instance, the bigram model (n=2) predicts the occurrence of a word given only its previous word, while the trigram model (n=3) predicts the occurrence of a word based on the previous two words. Even though the trigram model may be useful as it could predict sequences of words that have better medical meaning in terms of interpretability (ex. *500mg of paracetamol* (In English)), it may not be practical as it can increase the number of parameters and also the dimensionality of feature space.

The final approach is to assign a tf*idf weighting to all terms. *tf* is the simple term frequency; *idf* assigns in each term a weight such that it can compensate for the words that occur too often in the document, as they can be important to discriminate between others (Schütze et al., 2008). The number of features are reduced to a maximum of 500 terms, those with the highest tf*idf scores. A motivation for *tf*idf* was found in (Ehrentraut et al., 2016) where they utilized tf*idf, to classify healthcare associated infections and this method yielded the best results while extracting the most relevant results.

4.4. Classification

Three algorithms are benchmarked to evaluate the performance of the used methods :

- **RF**: Random Forests with 100 trees, gini impurity as the split criterion and the number of features considered at decision split criterion set to default$\sqrt{m}$ where m is the number of features in each dataset;
- **SVMlinear**: Support Vector Machines using a linear kernel and weighted class balance;
- **SVMrbf**: Support Vector Machines using the RBF kernel and weighted class balance;

4.5. Evaluation

All models were trained in the four different word sequences and for the three different window sizes. Stratified ten-fold cross validation was used, as described in (Kohavi, 1995) to ensure more efficient use of data. Since the datasets in this study are imbalanced, the Area Under the ROC Curve (AUC) was considered to be the most appropriate measure, as it has been proved to be an appropriate evaluation for skewed classification problems (Fawcett, 2006). Nevertheless, as in some cases the class imbalance favors the negative examples, the metrics precision, recall (as described in (Van Rijsbergen, 1979)) and F1 score were used to evaluate the results of each class independently.

5. Results

Table 2 presents our results in terms of predictive modelling. Five different types of ADEs expressed in the following ICD-10 codes D61.1, E27.3, G62.0, L27.0 and T80.8 are investigated. The table is separated in three sub-tables that present the investigation of variable window sizes for each ADE. The columns present the investigation of unigrams, bigrams, trigrams and tf*idf, for each ADE and window size. The results are depicted as mean AUC. Table 3 presents a classification report for the best performing window size and word sequence method for each ADE. Reported are: precision, recall, F1 score and support for both positive and negative classes, for the previously mentioned ADEs. Note that in binary classification, recall of the positive class is also known as sensitivity; recall of the negative class is specificity. Finally, Table 4 compares our classification results to the approach by Bamba and Papapetrou (2019).

Word vector representation. First, we investigate the importance of different kind of representations in a word level, for each ADE. We observe that although all n-gram approaches perform well they are almost always outperformed by the *tf*idf* approach. Specifically, ADEs

E27.3, G62.0, L27.0 and T80.8 had better classification performance when considering the inverse document frequency (idf) with the SVM linear classifier. Comparing the n-grams, the unigram was always performing better than the bigram and trigram approaches (sequence of two and three adjacent words), where the results are anging from 2% to 9% improvement. Unigram was always the second best performing after tf*idf.

Window Sizes. The aim in this section is to investigate variable window sizes in the patient trajectory following the work of Bamba and Papapetrou (2019). We can see that L27.0 acquired better results in a small window size of 30 days and E27.3, T80.8 gave an improvement of 1% to 3% in a window size of 60 days as compared to 30 and 90 days. For ADEs D61.1 and G62.0 the best results are obtained in a 90 days patient history length with AUC 0.9542 and 0.9045 respectively.

Classification Report. Furthermore, for each best performing size and word vector representation we provide a classification report for both negative and positive classes. In Table 3, we observe that for the ADEs D61.1 and T80.8 where the class imbalance favors the positive class, the precision and recall are high. However, for ADEs E27.3 and G62.0 we can see that the classifier is not performing well in the positive class, failing both to retrieve and correctly classify the cases, as the class distribution is skewed towards the negative class.

Comparison to LDM approach. Finally, we compare our approach to the LDM framework as described in (Bamba and Papapetrou, 2019). In this paper the authors studied the importance of incorporating three different types of structured predictors in the learning process, Lab measurements, Drug codes, Diagnoses codes (LDM) while using variable window sizes. In table 4, depicted are the best performing windows sizes and classifiers for each of the approaches. We observe that for 4 out for 5 classifiers, employing features found in the clinical text improves the classification task. Specifically, there is an improvement of 1% for D61.1, 13% for E27.3, 2% for G62.0 and 15% for L27.0.

5.1. Important Features and Medical Relevance

In this section top textual features are provided that were found important by the SVM classifier, for two of the studied ADEs. We are interested in investigating the features that the classifier based its decision upon and additionally, see if the are medically relevant. We only consider the results from SVM linear classifier and use the weights obtained from the coefficients of the vector which are orthogonal to the hyperplane and their direction indicates the predicted class. The absolute size of the coefficients in relation to each other can then be used to determine feature importance for the data separation task.

In figures 2, 3 we observe the most important features for both the negative and positive classes as decided by the SVM linear classifier for ADEs D61.1 (drug induced aplastic anaemia) and L27.0 (drug induced generalized skin eruption). Among the most import features for D61.1 are the words (In Swedish but also translated to English in parenthesis) *thrombocyter (platelets), sandimmun (a drug), blodtransfusion (blood transfusion), cytostatica (cytostatics), lymfom (lymphoma)* and *crp (a protein in blood made by the liver).* For example, according to the literature, irregular levels of plateles in the blood are indicators of aplastic anaemia and a way to treat is by blood transfusions (NIDDK, 2019). For L27.0 among the most important features are *svullnad (swelling), mjölk (milk), ägg (egg), övre (upper), hudutslag (rash), nötter (nuts), andningsljud* (noises heard on auscultation over any part of the respiratory tract), *mildison* (cream prescribed to relieve skin inflammation and itching), *reagera (react), akuten (emergency unit), hb (hemoglobin), ser (look), stor (big)* and *remiss (referral).*

These words are highly relevant for each ADE studied, thus indicating that the model is not performing at random. Nevertheless, we can observe that words such as the abbreviation *pga (because of)* or the numerical value *14*, are considered important features but cannot be related to the ADEs at a first glance. In the future, it would be of great importance to incorporate a medical expert in the process in order to validate the procedure and results, so as to create a safe and interpretable prediction model. Additionally, we observe that in some of the ADEs, the top important features include drugs or diagnoses that are administered and registered after the manifestation of the ADE. This indicates that the adverse events might be registered in the record at a later point in time, thus capturing both the treatment and the diagnosis of the ADE.

6. Analysis

The increased adoption of Electronic EHRs has brought a tremendous increase in the quantities of health care data. They contain records that offer a holistic overview of a patient's medical history, rendering them a valuable tool source for drug safety surveillance. Machine learning methods can be employed to uncover clinical and medical insights stemming from both structured and unstructured data to detect ADEs. Existing approaches on ADE prediction from EHRs have been mainly focusing on utilizing structured data types, on the other hand, text mining techniques have focused on identifying ADEs globally rather than focusing on specific types that occur frequently. This paper followed the work of Bamba and Papapetrou (2019) and incorporated in the learning process textual features while considering variable window lengths, for the five most frequent ADEs found in the SU-ADE corpus.

The experimental findings suggest that the textual features contain information that is highly important for ADE prediction. We observe that in many cases the word predictors outperformed the framework by Bamba and Papapetrou (2019) where the only utilized structured lab measurements, diagnoses and medication codes. In section 5.1 we included a number of important predictors as found by the SVM linear classifier, indicating that the model is not performing at random. We observed that some of

	unigram			bigram			trigram			tf*idf		
	RF	svmLin	svmRbf	RF	svmLin	svmRbf	RF	svmLin	svmRbf	RF	svmLin	svmRbf
30 DAYS												
D61.1	0.9330	0.8707	0.8780	0.9159	0.8504	0.9133	0.8630	0.7604	0.8179	**0.9408**	0.9432	0.9249
E27.3	0.8109	0.7466	0.7113	0.6970	0.6928	0.7384	0.6947	0.7481	0.7272	0.7985	**0.8700**	0.8630
G62.0	0.7875	0.7436	**0.8805**	0.6879	0.6871	0.7796	0.6777	0.6833	0.7002	0.8235	0.8268	0.8666
L27.0	0.9272	0.8491	0.9118	0.8863	0.8328	0.8811	0.8113	0.8145	0.7920	0.9226	0.9109	0.9031
T80.8	0.8929	0.8173	0.8871	0.8829	0.8168	0.8621	0.8221	0.8105	0.8339	0.8863	**0.9060**	0.8962
60DAYS												
D61.1	0.9354	0.8632	0.8572	0.9369	0.8882	0.9025	0.8597	0.7585	0.8477	0.9415	**0.9502**	0.9275
E27.3	0.8224	0.7941	0.7567	0.7574	0.766	0.7674	0.7040	0.7294	0.7194	0.8626	0.8822	0.8677
G62.0	0.8382	0.7603	0.828	0.7660	0.7301	0.8467	0.7490	0.721	0.7956	0.8547	0.8742	**0.8829**
L27.0	**0.9206**	0.8408	0.9089	0.8882	0.8303	0.8862	0.8134	0.8083	0.7997	0.9120	0.9108	0.8936
T80.8	0.9076	0.8274	0.8865	0.9042	0.8304	0.8887	0.8581	0.8609	0.8691	0.9185	0.9207	0.9171
90DAYS												
D61.1	0.9403	0.8933	0.8503	0.9245	0.8836	0.8980	0.8651	0.8128	0.8425	0.9424	0.9542	0.9352
E27.3	0.7833	0.7647	0.7367	0.7219	0.6886	0.7259	0.6748	0.6848	0.6912	0.8078	**0.8420**	0.8337
G62.0	0.8357	0.7902	0.8454	0.8000	0.7639	0.8666	0.7749	0.7341	0.8048	0.8788	0.9045	0.8892
L27.0	**0.9216**	0.8427	0.9085	0.8811	0.824	0.8834	0.8248	0.7995	0.8036	0.9165	0.9142	0.8941
T80.8	0.8984	0.7936	0.8565	0.8801	0.8172	0.8856	0.8623	0.8447	0.8654	0.8836	**0.9005**	0.8944

Table 2: AUC obtained by 3 classifiers on 3 different patient history lengths for 5 different ADE cases and 4 different word weighting factor approaches. Each table presents the AUC obtained by stratified 10-fold cross validation on the different window sizes. In bold: best AUC for each ADE in the specific window size across all approaches, In red: Best AUC for the specific ADE across all window sizes, classifiers, and approaches;

	Class	Precision	Recall	F1 score
D61.1	Negative	0.78	0.80	0.79
	Positive	0.90	0.89	0.89
E27.3	Negative	0.95	0.85	0.89
	Positive	0.28	0.56	0.37
G62.0	Negative	0.98	0.91	0.94
	Positive	0.30	0.62	0.40
L27.0	Negative	0.89	0.83	0.86
	Positive	0.72	0.82	0.77
T80.8	Negative	0.70	0.79	0.74
	Positive	0.93	0.89	0.91

Table 3: Classification report of each ADE in the best performing classifier and window size for each of them (the ones reported as red in Table 2). Support: the number of occurrences of each class in the correct values

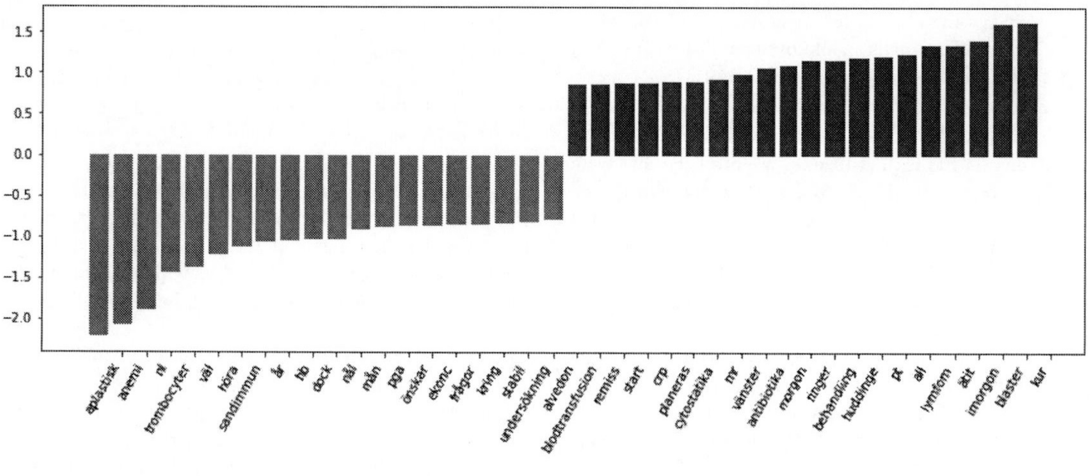

Figure 2: Top 20 feature importance for D61.1 in a 90 days window size using the tf*idf weighting and SVM linear. X-axis: Feature words in Swedish, Y-axis: Vector coefficients.

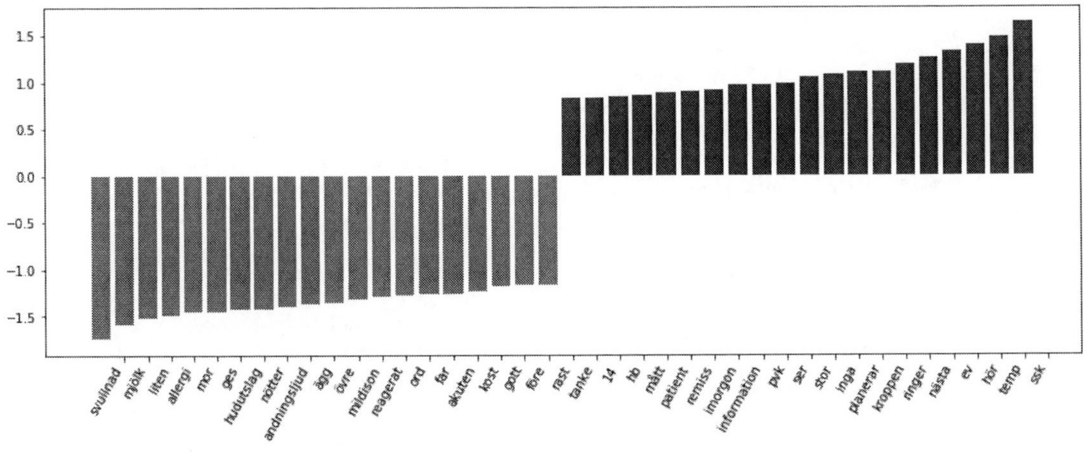

Figure 3: Top 20 feature importance for L27.0 in a 30 days window size using the tf*idf weighting and SVM linear. X-axis: Feature words in Swedish, Y-axis: Vector coefficients

	tf*idf	LDM	WS
D61.1	0.954	0.948	90
E27.3	0.882	0.756	30
G62.0	0.904	0.880	90
L27.0	0.927	0774	60
T80.8	0.920	0.946	30

Table 4: Comparison of textual tf*idf and LDM (Labs, Diagnoses, Medication) approach. WS: Best Performing Window Size for each ADE

the features are highly relevant with each ADE studied; for L27.0 (drug induced skin eruption) important features were swelling, egg and nuts or rash. This indicated that incorporating the clinical text in the learning process can provide medically sound predictions and provide a more interpretable model. Moreover, we observed that, as proposed by (Ehrentraut et al., 2016), tf*idf yields reasonably good results that can be clinically interpreted. Finally, the results indicate that considering different patient history lengths can increase the classification performance by 3%. A long patient history length could add noise to the dataset, while a short one could eradicate very important information. Carefully studying the appropriate window length depending on the ADE of interest is very important as it can provide medically relevant predictions.

A limitation of this study is the formulation of the ADE positive and negative groups. Although the positive groups are based on the study by (Stausberg and Hasford, 2011) the negative cases seem tightly close to the positive ones. Someone could argue that as some ADE codes are very similar to each other they can be used interchangeably by medical experts. Moreover, another limitation is the distribution of the positive and negative examples. In some datasets the distribution of the positive examples is far less than the one of the negative examples, causing lower predictive performance.

For future work we would like to investigate other ways of defining the control and test groups for the ADE examples. Furthermore, we would like to incorporate all structured and unstructured features in the learning process; we believe that not only it will improve the model performance but it will also shed light in ADE signalling. A natural extension of this paper would be to implement more recent NLP techniques as well as word-embeddings and evaluate them on the ADE problem. We plan to use decompounding of words to see if the performance of our algorithms will improve analysing the decompounded elements. Lastly, an extension would be to dynamically adjust the window sizes for each patient or ADE studied.

7. Conclusion

This paper focused on utilizing textual features using different word sequences and patient history lengths to predict ADEs from EHRs. We demonstrated the importance of incorporating in the machine learning process clinical text, as this textual source are very informative towards ADE prediction. NLP techniques can be utilized to meet the challenges posed by narrative data and provide meaningful predictions.

Acknowledgements

We would like to thank professor Panos Papapetrou for insightful advices regarding the machine learning set up.

Bibliographical References

Bagattini, F., Karlsson, I., Rebane, J., and Papapetrou, P. (2019). A classification framework for exploiting sparse multi-variate temporal features with application to adverse drug event detection in medical records. *BMC Medical Informatics and Decision Making*, 19(1):7, 12.

Bamba, M. and Papapetrou, P. (2019). Mining Adverse Drug Events Using Multiple Feature Hierarchies and Patient History Windows. In *Proceedings of the Workshop on Data Mining in Biomedical Informatics and Healthcare DMBIH'19 in conjunction with IEEE International Conference on Data Mining (ICDM'19), Beijing.*

Carlberger, J., Dalianis, H., Hassel, M., and Knutsson, O. (2001). Improving precision in information retrieval for swedish using stemming. In *Proceedings of the 13th Nordic Conference of Computational Linguistics (NODALIDA 2001).*

Dalianis, H., Henriksson, A., Kvist, M., Velupillai, S., and Weegar, R. (2015). HEALTH BANK–A Workbench for Data Science Applications in Healthcare. In *Proceedings of the CAiSE-2015 Industry Track co-located with 27th Conference on Advanced Information Systems Engineering (CAiSE 2015), J. Krogstie, G. Juel-Skielse and V. Kabilan, (Eds.), Stockholm, Sweden, June 11, 2015, CEUR, Vol-1381*, pages 1–18.

Ehrentraut, C., Ekholm, M., Tanushi, H., Tiedemann, J., and Dalianis, H. (2016). Detecting hospital-acquired infections: a document classification approach using support vector machines and gradient tree boosting. *Health informatics journal*, 24(1):24–42.

Eriksson, R., Jensen, P. B., Frankild, S., Jensen, L. J., and Brunak, S. (2013). Dictionary construction and identification of possible adverse drug events in Danish clinical narrative text. *Journal of the American Medical Informatics Association : JAMIA*, 20(5):947–53.

Fawcett, T. (2006). An introduction to ROC analysis. *Pattern Recognition Letters*, 27(8):861–874, 6.

Harpaz, R., Haerian, K., Chase, H. S., and Friedman, C. (2010). Mining electronic health records for adverse drug effects using regression based methods. In *the 1st ACM International Health Informatics Symposium*, pages 100–107. ACM.

Henriksson, A., Zhao, J., Boström, H., and Dalianis, H. (2015). Modeling electronic health records in ensembles of semantic spaces for adverse drug event detection. In *Proceedings - 2015 IEEE International Conference on Bioinformatics and Biomedicine, BIBM 2015*, pages 343–350. Institute of Electrical and Electronics Engineers Inc., dec.

Henriksson, A. (2015). Representing Clinical Notes for Adverse Drug Event Detection. pages 152–158. Proceedings of the Sixth International Workshop on Health Text Mining and Information Analysis / [ed] Cyril Grouin, Thierry Hamon, Aurélie Névéol, Pierre Zweigenbaum, Association for Computational Linguistics, 2015, s. 152-158.

Karimi, S., Wang, C., Metke-Jimenez, A., Gaire, R., and Paris, C. (2015). Text and data mining techniques in adverse drug reaction detection. *ACM Computing Surveys (CSUR)*, 47(4):56.

Kohavi, R. (1995). A Study of Cross-Validation and Bootstrap for Accuracy Estimation and Model Selection. In *International Joint Conference on Artificial Intelligence (IJCAI)*, pages 1137–1145.

LePendu, P., Iyer, S. V., Bauer-Mehren, A., Harpaz, R., Mortensen, J. M., Podchiyska, T., Ferris, T. A., and Shah, N. H. (2013). Pharmacovigilance using clinical notes. *Clinical Pharmacology and Therapeutics*, 93(6):547–555, jun.

Manning, C. D., Manning, C. D., and Schütze, H. (1999). *Foundations of statistical natural language processing*. MIT press.

Melton, G. B. and Hripcsak, G. (2005). Automated detection of adverse events using natural language processing of discharge summaries. *Journal of the American Medical Informatics Association*, 12(4):448–457.

NIDDK. (2019). Aplastic Anemia & Myelodysplastic Syndromes. `https://www.niddk.nih.gov/health-information/blood-diseases/aplastic-anemia-myelodysplastic-syndromes`, Accessed: 2019-11-21.

Park, M. Y., Yoon, D., Lee, K., Kang, S. Y., Park, I., Lee, S.-H., Kim, W., Kam, H. J., Lee, Y.-H., Kim, J. H., and Park, R. W. (2011). A novel algorithm for detection of adverse drug reaction signals using a hospital electronic medical record database. *Pharmacoepidemiology and Drug Safety*, 20(6):598–607.

Schütze, H., Manning, C. D., and Raghavan, P. (2008). Introduction to information retrieval. In *Proceedings of the international communication of association for computing machinery conference*, page 260.

Stausberg, J. and Hasford, J. (2011). Drug-related admissions and hospital-acquired adverse drug events in Germany: A longitudinal analysis from 2003 to 2007 of ICD-10-coded routine data. *BMC Health Services Research*, 11.

Van Rijsbergen, C. (1979). *Information Retrieval*. Butterworth & Co. Accessed 2018-01-11.

Wang, X., Hripcsak, G., Markatou, M., and Friedman, C. (2009). Active Computerized Pharmacovigilance Using Natural Language Processing, Statistics, and Electronic Health Records: A Feasibility Study. *Journal of the American Medical Informatics Association*, 16(3):328–337, May.

Weiskopf, N. G., Hripcsak, G., Swaminathan, S., and Weng, C. (2013). Defining and measuring completeness of electronic health records for secondary use. *Journal of Biomedical Informatics*, 46(5):830–836, Oct.

Zhao, J., Henriksson, A., and Böstrom, H. (2014). Detecting Adverse Drug Events Using Concept Hierarchies of Clinical Codes. pages 285–293, 9.

Zhao, J., Henriksson, A., Asker, L., and Boström, H. (2015a). Predictive modeling of structured electronic health records for adverse drug event detection. *BMC Medical Informatics and Decision Making*, 15(Suppl 4):S1.

Zhao, J., Henriksson, A., and Boström, H. (2015b). Cascading adverse drug event detection in electronic health records. In *2015 IEEE International Conference on Data Science and Advanced Analytics (DSAA)*, pages 1–8. IEEE, 10.

Zhao, J., Henriksson, A., Kvist, M., Asker, L., and Boström, H. (2015c). Handling Temporality of Clinical Events for Drug Safety Surveillance. *Annual Symposium proceedings. AMIA Symposium*, 2015:1371–80.

Proceedings of MultilingualBIO 2020, pages 9–14
Language Resources and Evaluation Conference (LREC 2020), Marseille, 11–16 May 2020

Building a Norwegian Lexical Resource for Medical Entity Recognition

Ildikó Pilán[*], Pål H. Brekke[†], Lilja Øvrelid[*]
[*]Department of Informatics, University of Oslo, [†]Department of Cardiology, Oslo University Hospital Rikshospitalet
Oslo, Norway
ildikop@ifi.uio.no, pabrek@ous-hf.no, liljao@ifi.uio.no

Abstract

We present a large Norwegian lexical resource of categorized medical terms. The resource merges information from large medical databases, and contains over 77,000 unique entries, including automatically mapped terms from a Norwegian medical dictionary. We describe the methodology behind this automatic dictionary entry mapping based on keywords and suffixes and further present the results of a manual evaluation performed on a subset by a domain expert. The evaluation indicated that ca. 80% of the mappings were correct.

Keywords: lexical resource, medical terminology, Named Entity Recognition, clinical text, Norwegian

1. Introduction

Named Entity Recognition (NER) is a common task within the area of clinical Natural Language Processing (NLP) with the aim of extracting critical information such as diseases and treatments from unstructured texts (Friedman et al., 1994; Xu et al., 2010; Jagannatha and Yu, 2016).

Current neural approaches to NER typically require a large amount of annotated data for a reliable performance (Ma and Hovy, 2016; Lample et al., 2016). Distant supervision (Mintz et al., 2009), however, relaxes this constraint on the training data size thanks to the combined use of information from lexical resources, a small amount of training data and large amounts of raw data. This technique has been successfully applied also in the biomedical and clinical domain (Fries et al., 2017; Shang et al., 2018). In absence of even a small amount of annotated data, categorized lexical resources can also be used as gazetteers in rule-based approaches.

There is currently no large and freely available lexical resource with categorized entity types for Norwegian medical terms to be used for clinical NER with distant supervision. This paper presents an effort to create such a resource by collecting and merging lists of terms available from a number of other smaller and more specialized resources. We implement and describe an automatic mapping method which is applied to a dictionary containing a variety of definitions for relevant terms and present an evaluation of this mapping using both inter-resource overlap and manual evaluation performed by a domain expert. The resulting lexical resource will be made freely available.

2. Background

Medical Entity Recognition often makes use of lexical resources such as lists of disease names derived from the International Statistical Classification of Diseases and Related Health Problems (ICD) resource (World Health Organization and others, 2004) or from disease information from general resources, such as the Medical Subject Headings (Lipscomb, 2000, MeSH). There has been quite a bit of work aimed at creating semantic lexicons for use in NLP from such domain-specific resources (Johnson, 1999; Liu et al., 2012).

Automated extraction of medical entities from clinical text has been the topic of several research efforts more recently, a majority aimed at English (Xu et al., 2010; Jagannatha and Yu, 2016) and Chinese clinical text (Wu et al., 2018). For a language that is very closely related to Norwegian, Skeppstedt et al. (2014) developed and evaluated an entity detection system for Findings, Disorders and Body Parts in Swedish. In order to alleviate the need for manual annotation, distant supervision has recently been applied also to entity recognition in the medical domain for English and Chinese (Shang et al., 2018; Nooralahzadeh et al., 2019).

3. Norwegian Medical Terminology Resources

There are a number of resources which contain Norwegian medical terms that could in principle be relevant for NER.

The *Medisinsk ordbok* (MO) 'Medical Dictionary' (Nylenna, 1990) contains 23,863 Norwegian medical terms of various kinds including, among others, names of diseases and treatments, anatomical terminology as well as types of medical specialists and specialization areas. The dictionary contains synonyms and one or more definitions of these terms depending on the number of senses per entry.

Other rich sources of Norwegian medical terms and their corresponding standardized codes are available from the website of *Directoratet for e-helse* 'Norwegian Directorate for e-health'. One is the Norwegian equivalent of the 10th Revision of ICD (ICD-10). The widely-used resource lists both coarse and fine-grained codes and corresponding terms relative to diseases, symptoms and findings. Another source is the Procedure Coding Schemes list (referred to as PROC here), which includes diagnostic, medical and surgical intervention names and codes (Direktoratet for e-helse, 2020). Moreover, Laboratoriekodeverket[1] 'List of laboratory codes' (LABV) contains various substance names relevant in laboratory analyses. The web page of this list also includes a shorter list of anatomical locations, which we refer to as ALOC here. Yet another resource available from the Directorate's web site is the Norwegian equivalent of

[1]https://ehelse.no/kodeverk/laboratoriekodeverket

the International Classification of Primary Care (ICPC-2), which includes diagnosis terms as well as health problem and medical procedure names.

The FEST (*Forskrivnings- og ekspedisjonsstøtte*, 'Prescribing and dispensing support') database[2] contains information about all medicines and other goods that can be prescribed in Norway. FEST is a publicly available resource published by *Statens legemiddelverk* 'The Norwegian Medicines Agency'.

Rama et al. (2018) present a corpus of synthetically produced clinical statements about family history in Norwegian (here dubbed FAM-HIST). The corpus is annotated with clinical entities relating to family history, such as Family Member, Condition and Event, as well as relations between these.

4. Automatic Dictionary Entry Mapping Method

The use of dictionary definitions as a source of semantic information has been the topic of quite a bit of research in lexical semantics, from the early work of Markowitz et al. (1986) where patterns in the dictionary definitions along with suffix information gave rise to a semantic lexicon to more recent efforts to embed dictionary definitions in order to derive semantic categories for phrasal units (Hill et al., 2016).

In this work, we map entries from the MO dictionary to categories, i.e. to medical entity types. We identify 12 different types of entity categories based on previous work (Zhang and Elhadad, 2013) and the inspection of MO entries. We then implement a rule-based mapping method relying on suffixes and keywords.

4.1. Mapping Strategies

The mapping method consists of four different mapping strategies: two relying on the entries themselves and two deriving the mapped category from the definitions. One of these is suffix based, the others operate based on keywords. In what follows, we describe each of these strategies in detail.

Suffix-based mapping (*strategy SUFF*) This strategy consists of mapping an entry to a category whenever its last characters match a specific suffix. Many medical terms have Greek or Latin origin resulting in suffixes that give rather clear indications of the category of an entry. We compile a list of suffixes based on both frequently occurring suffixes in the data and an online resource[3]. We only include suffixes and endings which can be mapped to an unambiguous category in the majority of cases. The complete list used for the mapping is presented in Table 1.

Keyword-based mapping Mapping entries to keywords is primarily used to map an entry to a category based on the first noun occurring in their definition (*strategy KW-1N*). To be able to detect first nouns, definitions are tokenized and part-of-speech tagged with UDPipe (Straka et al., 2016).

[2] https://legemiddelverket.no/andre-temaer/fest

[3] https://en.wikipedia.org/wiki/List_of_medical_roots,_suffixes_and_prefixes

Category	Suffixes
CONDITION	-agi, -algi, -algia, -blastom, -cele, -cytose, -donti, -dynia, -emi, -emia, -epsi, -ism, -isme, -ismus, -itis, -oma, -pati, -plasi, -plegi, -ruptur, -sarkom, -sis, -trofi, -temi, -toni, -tropi
DISCIPLINE	-iatri, -logi
MICROORG	-coccus, -bacillus, -bacter
PERSON	-iater, -olog
PROCEDURE	-biopsi, -grafi, -metri, -skopi, -tomi
SUBSTANCE	-cillin
TOOL	-graf, -meter, -skop

Table 1: Suffix mapping.

To create a list of keywords for the mapping, we inspect the 200 most frequent nouns in the definitions and manually map the ones with a strong indication of a single category. We complement this with other frequent nouns which can be good indicators of a category. This results in a list of 168 mapped keywords, see Table 2 for some examples.

When mapping, we require the first noun of a definition to either (i) exactly match a keyword or (ii) to contain it. The latter is only applied for keywords longer than 4 characters to avoid short sequences which might over-generate false positives (e.g. *tap* 'loss' for *katapleksi* 'cataplexy'). When checking for contained keyword, we limit the position of the keyword match to the second character onward in the first noun to approximate the occurrence of a keyword as the second part of a compound as this is more indicative of categories. Given that many dictionary entries are also compounds, we apply the mapping based on contained keyword also to the entries themselves (*strategy KW-E*).

When applying keyword-based mapping to definitions, before detecting the first noun, we remove those nouns and phrases which have little added semantic value relevant for the category. These include prepositional phrases forming a complex noun phrase typical of definitions (e.g. *form av* 'form of'), nouns not indicative of a category (e.g. *uttrykk* 'expression') and abbreviations (*plur.* 'plural', *lat.* 'Latin').

During the mapping procedure, first each strategy casts a vote on the category. In case of multiple votes with a disagreement, the category is based on a single mapping strategy chosen following a specific order, starting from the strategy with the highest expected precision and continuing with the ones with increasingly high recall as follows: SUFF $\rightarrow$ KW-E $\rightarrow$ KW-1N. After a first iteration of mapping, we perform a second iteration and map uncategorized entries if there is an entry already mapped available for the first noun in their definition (*strategy ITER*).

The MO resource contains altogether 2,387 synonyms, which were treated as separate entries with the same definition. The number of entries with multiple meanings (and definitions) were merely 360 in total, amounting to 1.5%. Since such polysemous entries were so rare, we consider only the first sense of each entry.

The methodology outlined above could be applied also for categorizing medical terminology in other languages via, for example, machine translating the list of keywords

Category	Description	Example keywords	Mapped entry examples
ABBREV	abbreviations, acronyms	*forkortelse* 'abbreviation'	*Ahus, ADH*
ANAT-LOC	anatomical locations	*celler* 'cells', *muskel* 'muscle', *kroppsdel* 'bodypart'	*fødselskanalen* 'birth-channel', *halsmusklene* 'throat-muscles'
CONDITION	diseases, findings	*sykdom* 'disease', *tilstand* 'condition', *mangel* 'deficiency'	*leukemi* 'leukemia', *leverkoma* 'hepatic coma'
DISCIPLINE	medical disciplines	*studium* 'study', *forskning* 'research', *teori* 'theory'	*dietetikk* 'diethetics', *biomekanikk* 'biomechanics'
MICROORG	microorganisms of different kind	*bakterie* 'bacteoria', *organisme* 'organism', *virus* 'virus'	*kolibakterie* 'colibacteria', *blodparasitter* 'blood parasites'
ORGANIZATION	institutions and organizations	*foretak* 'company', *institutt* 'institute'	*Røde Kors* 'Red Cross', *sanatorium* 'sanatorium'
PERSON	types of practitioner or patient	*lege* 'doctor', *pasient* 'patient', *individ* 'individual'	*myop* 'myope', *nevrolog* 'neurologist'
PHYSIOLOGY	physiological functions	*refleks* 'reflex', *sammentrekning* 'contraction'	*adsorpsjon* 'absorption', *forbrenning* 'burning'
PROCEDURE	procedure and treatment types	*behandling* 'treatment', *fjerning* 'removal'	*nyrebiopsi* 'kidney biopsy', *detoksifisering* 'detoxification'
SERVICE	types of services	*tjeneste* 'service', *omsorg* 'care'	*tannhelsetjeneste*, ' dental service', *sjelesorg* 'counseling'
SUBSTANCE	medicines and other substances	*stoff* 'substance', *løsning* 'solution' *medikament* 'drug'	*aspartam* 'aspartam', *paracetamol* 'paracetamol'
TOOL	instruments and tools	*instrument* 'instrument', *verktøy* 'tool'	*diatermikniv* 'diathermy blade', *defibrillator* 'defibrillator'

Table 2: List of entity type categories, keywords and mapped entries.

(or terms) used and making small language-specific orthographic adjustments to the suffix mappings from Table 1. Such suffixes are often adapted to the orthographic conventions of a certain language, as also Grigonytė et al. (2016) found in the case of Swedish.

5. Mapping Results

The results of the category mapping for MO based on the methodology outlined in Section 4. is presented in Table 3.

Category	# entries
CONDITION	5,522
SUBSTANCE	2,216
PROCEDURE	1,467
DISCIPLINE	418
ANAT-LOC	408
PERSON	282
MICROORG	227
ABBREV	216
TOOL	210
PHYSIOLOGY	132
ORGANIZATION	81
SERVICE	48
Total mapped	**11,227**
Not mapped	12,636
Total	**23,863**

Table 3: Mapping results for MO.

The percentage of mapped entries was 47%, almost half of all available entries in MO. The other terms, which were not mapped, did not match either any of the suffixes or the keywords used. The latter includes, among others, cases where the first noun in the definition was a synonym of the term and hence too specific to be included in the list of keywords used (e.g. the term *klorose* 'chlorosis', a type of anemia occurring mosty in adolescent girls is defined using *jomfrusyk* 'virgin sick').

Based on some manual inspection, most non-mapped terms would fit one of the categories proposed, with few exceptions that might lead to rather small categories, such as regulations (e.g. *internasjonalt helsereglement* 'international health regulations'). Several non-mapped terms should belong to the ANAT-LOC category. The proposed keyword-based methods would often be ambiguous for these terms and could indicate either an anatomical location or a medical condition related to it. For example, both the ANAT-LOC *hjertekammer* 'ventricle' and the CONDITION *panserhjerte* 'armoured heart' contain the keyword *hjerte* 'heart' and have this word also as the first noun in their definition, their category could thus not be determined by our method. Additional databases containing a detailed list of anatomical location terms are therefore particularly useful for expanding our resource.

We also inspected the distribution of the mapping strategies used (see Table 4), where MULTI stands for a category selected based on the unanimous vote of multiple voting strategies. We can observe that the most frequently used strategy was KW-IN. Mappings based on multiple voting strategies selecting the same category were also rather common, occurring in 21% of all mapped entries.

Strategy	# entries
KW-1N	5,489
MULTI	2,397
ITER	1,157
SUFF	1,096
KW-E	1,088
Total	**11,227**

Table 4: Distribution of mapping strategy use.

6. Resource Merging

The mapped MO entries were complemented with data from the other resources described in Section 3. The mapping for these resources was straightforward since each resource contained either one specific type of entity or manual annotation was available.

At a closer inspection, we found that the ALOC list contains, besides anatomic locations, several terms which could belong to more than one category depending on the context of their use, e.g. *tracheostomi* 'tracheostomy' could either be ANAT-LOC referring to the hole created during a tracheostomy or it could refer to the procedure itself. These cases were mapped to PROC for reasons of consistency with the suffix-based mapping applied, but it might be worth to accommodate multiple categories in future versions. This list has been manually revised by a medical expert who disambiguated the category consistently with the mapping methodology used.

From FAM-HIST, we collected all occurrences of condition and event entities and mapped them to our CONDITION category. The SUBSTANCE category was augmented, in part, based on the FEST resource. The terms collected from FEST included substance names (also in English, when available) as well as medical product names with and without strength information. From ICD-10, both the disease names corresponding to the 3 and the 4 digit codes were preserved. Only 16% of the ICD codes were 3 digit codes.

From ICPC-2, we included all terms, sub-terms and short forms under the CONDITION category except for the terms appearing in the *Procedure codes* chapter, which were mapped to the PROCEDURE category. Terms from the *Social problems* chapter were excluded as most of these were not strictly speaking medical conditions (e.g. *lav inntekt* 'low income'). We observed a minor difference compared to ICD between some terms associated to the same code (e.g. *Blindtarmsbetennelse* vs. *Uspesifisert appendisitt* for code K37, appendicitis).

In the case of LABV, we included under the SUBSTANCE category all substance names, medicine and other medical product names and brands together with type and strength information when available (e.g. *Kortison Tab 25 mg* 'Cortisone Tablet 25 mg'). Lastly, all codes from PROC were included without any filtering.

Table 5 presents the amount of total entries available from various resources compared to MO. The total number of categorized entries created after merging and excluding all inter-resource overlaps was 78,105 with the original casing and 77,320 when normalizing all entries to lowercase.

Resource	Category	# entries
MO	Multiple	11,227
ALOC	Multiple	287
FAM-HIST	COND.	283
FEST	SUBST.	26,234
ICD-10	COND.	10,765
ICPC-2	Multiple	9,420
LABV	SUBST.	14,193
PROC	PROC.	8,883
Total	N/A	**81,292**

Table 5: Number and type of entries in different resources.

7. Resource-based Automatic Evaluation

Thanks to a certain amount of overlap between the mapped MO entries and the other resources, we can use information from the latter to automatically evaluate the former. Table 6 shows the overlap and the percentage of correct mappings.

Resource	# overlap	Correct (%)	Category
ALOC	33	57.6	Multiple
FAM-HIST	22	63.6	COND.
FEST	744	97.3	SUBST.
ICD-10	307	97.7	COND.
ICPC-2	886	94.0	Multiple
LABV	297	85.5	SUBST.
PROC	89	97.8	PROC.

Table 6: Evaluation results of the mapped MO entries.

On average, 85% mappings were correct out of the total of 2,378 overlapping terms from the resources listed in Table 6. Approximately 21% of all mapped terms from MO were thus evaluated (and corrected) automatically with the help of the other resources. Most misclassifications occurred with the ALOC and FAM-HIST resources and concerned the ANAT-LOC and CONDITION categories.

8. Manual Evaluation

Given that the overlap between MO and the other resources was limited to certain categories, we further performed a manual evaluation of the automatically mapped MO entries in order to assess their quality.

We randomly selected 1,128 terms to evaluate manually, aiming at a balanced amount per category (100 each) and mapping method. We included all available terms for categories where the total amount of terms remained below 100. The terms were categorized by a medical expert without access to the automatically mapped categories and the mapping method used. We present the per-category precision and recall in Table 7, where the number of terms in the last column refers to manually assigned labels.

112 terms were labeled as 'OTHER' in cases where a term did not belong to any of the 12 categories indicated or when terms were outside of the area of expertise of the evaluator. Table 7 excludes OTHER, as this was not part of the automatically mapped categories. The percentage of correctly categorized entries including and excluding terms la-

Category	Prec	Recall	#
ABBREV	0.969	0.750	124
ANAT-LOC	0.928	0.796	113
CONDITION	0.915	0.623	138
DISCIPLINE	0.702	0.855	69
MICROORG	0.871	0.976	83
ORGANIZATION	0.548	0.714	56
PERSON	0.593	0.923	52
PHYSIOLOGY	0.710	0.815	81
PROCEDURE	0.793	0.821	84
SERVICE	0.667	0.468	47
SUBSTANCE	0.809	0.905	84
TOOL	0.846	0.906	85
Total	**0.779**	**0.796**	**1,016**
ORG+SER	0.830	0.854	103
Total ORG+SER	**0.815**	**0.839**	**1,016**

Table 7: Manual evaluation results.

beled as OTHER, was 71.5% and 79.4% respectively. In 20 cases, SERVICE and ORGANIZATION were indicated as alternative labels to each other. We therefore compute evaluation measures also with these two categories merged (ORG+SER). This yields in total 82% correct labels when excluding OTHER.
According to the confusion matrix in Figure 1, most automatic categorization errors occurred between CONDITION and PHYSIOLOGY. (SERVICE was mapped to ORGANIZATION here.)

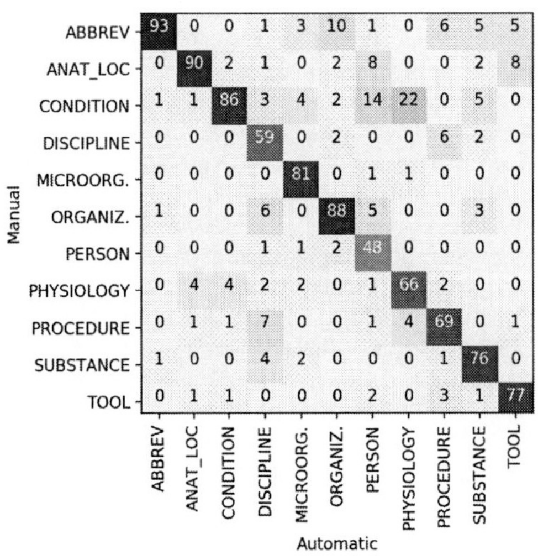

Figure 1: Confusion matrix over categories.

Errors related to the PERSON category were mostly connected to the use of *person* as keyword with the KW-E strategy, which generated false positives such as *schizoid personlighetstype* 'schizoid personality type'. Some categorization errors occurred because of the lack of prefix information, e.g. in the case of the keyword *refleks* 'reflex' in *arefleksi* 'areflexia' and *hyperrefleksi* 'hyperreflexia', which were both mapped to PHYSIOLOGY instead of CONDITION. This indicates that taking into consideration prefixes would contribute to improving the automatic categorization, especially for the KW-E strategy. The category label confusions between TOOL and ANAT-LOC originated from the keyword *apparat*, which proved to be ambiguous for the proposed categories, not only meaning 'device' and thus mappable to TOOL, but also meaning 'apparatus, system' as in *immunapparatet* 'immune system' and thus belonging to ANAT-LOC.
Most correct mappings (88.3%) with a single strategy were obtained using suffixed (SUFF), followed by the keyword mapping from first nouns (KW-1N, 79.9%) and entries (KW-E, 76.6%). The iterative mapping (ITER) yielded considerably fewer correct mappings, only 64.7%. When multiple strategies opted for the same category label, 98.2% of terms were correctly categorized.
As a final step during the resource creation, we revised the automatic categories based on the manually assigned ones. The updated count of terms per category in the resource after merging with other databases (eliminating overlap) and incorporating the evaluation results is reported in Table 8.

Category	# entries
SUBSTANCE	41,365
CONDITION	24,071
PROCEDURE	10,420
ANAT-LOC	658
DISCIPLINE	387
ABBREV	236
PERSON	232
TOOL	216
MICROORGANISM	193
OTHER	112
PHYSIOLOGY	112
ORGANIZATION	103
Total (original casing)	**78,105**

Table 8: Final term counts per category in the resource.

9. Conclusion

We introduced the first Norwegian lexical resource of categorized medical entities and provided an overview of the process of its creation. The resource unites information from medical databases as well as entries automatically mapped from a medical lexicon. A manual evaluation of a subset of the mapped terms confirmed that the automatic mappings were of a suitable quality to be used as additional supervision signal with machine learning based NER approaches. In future work we plan to apply the resource in medical entity recognition for Norwegian, using it to provide initial categories for distant supervision. We also plan to perform annotations with multiple raters and measure inter-annotator agreement for the proposed categories.

10. Acknowledgments

This work is funded by the Norwegian Research Council and more specifically by the BigMed project, an IKT-PLUSS Lighthouse project.

11. Bibliographical References

Direktoratet for e-helse. (2020). Prosedyrekodeverkene 'Procedure Coding Schemes'. `https://ehelse.no/kodeverk/prosedyrekodeverkene-kodeverk-for-medisinske-kirurgiske-og-radiologiske-prosedyrer-ncmp-ncsp-og-ncrp`. Accessed: 2020-02-10.

Friedman, C., Alderson, P. O., Austin, J. H., Cimino, J. J., and Johnson, S. B. (1994). A general natural-language text processor for clinical radiology. *Journal of the American Medical Informatics Association*, 1:161 – 174.

Fries, J. A., Wu, S., Ratner, A., and Ré, C. (2017). Swellshark: A generative model for biomedical named entity recognition without labeled data. *CoRR*, abs/1704.06360.

Grigonytė, G., Kvist, M., Wirén, M., Velupillai, S., and Henriksson, A. (2016). Swedification patterns of Latin and Greek affixes in clinical text. *Nordic Journal of Linguistics*, 39(1):5–37.

Hill, F., Cho, K., Korhonen, A., and Bengio, Y. (2016). Learning to understand phrases by embedding the dictionary. *Transactions of the Association for Computational Linguistics*, 4:17–30.

Jagannatha, A. N. and Yu, H. (2016). Bidirectional RNN for medical event detection in electronic health records. In *Proceedings of the 2016 Conference of the North American Chapter of the Association for Computational Linguistics: Human Language Technologies*, pages 473–482, San Diego, California, June. Association for Computational Linguistics.

Johnson, S. B. (1999). A semantic lexicon for medical language processing. *Journal of the American Medical Informatics Association*, 6(3):205–218.

Lample, G., Ballesteros, M., Subramanian, S., Kawakami, K., and Dyer, C. (2016). Neural architectures for named entity recognition. In *Proceedings of the 2016 Conference of the North American Chapter of the Association for Computational Linguistics: Human Language Technologies*, pages 260–270, San Diego, California, June. Association for Computational Linguistics.

Lipscomb, C. E. (2000). Medical subject headings (MeSH). *Bulletin of the Medical Library Association*, 88(3):265–266.

Liu, H., Wu, S. T., Li, D., Jonnalagadda, S., Sohn, S., Wagholikar, K., Haug, P. J., Huff, S. M., and Chute, C. G. (2012). Towards a semantic lexicon for clinical natural language processing. In *AMIA Annual Symposium Proceedings*, volume 2012, page 568. American Medical Informatics Association.

Ma, X. and Hovy, E. (2016). End-to-end sequence labeling via bi-directional LSTM-CNNs-CRF. In *Proceedings of the 54th Annual Meeting of the Association for Computational Linguistics (Volume 1: Long Papers)*, pages 1064–1074, Berlin, Germany, August. Association for Computational Linguistics.

Markowitz, J., Ahlswede, T., and Evens, M. (1986). Semantically significant patterns in dictionary definitions. In *Proceedings of the 24th annual meeting on Association for Computational Linguistics*, pages 112–119. Association for Computational Linguistics.

Mintz, M., Bills, S., Snow, R., and Jurafsky, D. (2009). Distant supervision for relation extraction without labeled data. In *Proceedings of the Joint Conference of the 47th Annual Meeting of the ACL and the 4th International Joint Conference on Natural Language Processing of the AFNLP: Volume 2 - Volume 2*, ACL '09, pages 1003–1011, Stroudsburg, PA, USA. Association for Computational Linguistics.

Nooralahzadeh, F., Lønning, J. T., and Øvrelid, L. (2019). Reinforcement-based denoising of distantly supervised NER with partial annotation. In *Proceedings of the 2nd Workshop on Deep Learning Approaches for Low-Resource NLP (DeepLo 2019)*, pages 225–233, Hong Kong, China, November. Association for Computational Linguistics.

Nylenna, M. (1990). *Medisinsk Ordbok*. Kunnskapsforlaget.

Rama, T., Brekke, P., Nytrø, Ø., and Øvrelid, L. (2018). Iterative development of family history annotation guidelines using a synthetic corpus of clinical text. In *Proceedings of the 9th International Workshop on Health Text Mining and Information Analysis (LOUHI 2018)*.

Shang, J., Liu, L., Ren, X., Gu, X., Ren, T., and Han, J. (2018). Learning named entity tagger using domain-specific dictionary. In *Proceedings of EMNLP*.

Skeppstedt, M., Kvist, M., Nilsson, G. H., and Dalianis, H. (2014). Automatic recognition of disorders, findings, pharmaceuticals and body structures from clinical text: An annotation and machine learning study. *Journal of Biomedical Informatics*, 49:148 – 158.

Straka, M., Hajic, J., and Straková, J. (2016). UDPipe: trainable pipeline for processing CoNLL-U files performing tokenization, morphological analysis, POS tagging and parsing. In *Proceedings of the Tenth International Conference on Language Resources and Evaluation (LREC'16)*, pages 4290–4297.

World Health Organization et al. (2004). ICD-10: International statistical classification of diseases and related health problems: Tenth revision.

Wu, Y., Jiang, M., Xu, J., Zhi, D., and Xu, H. (2018). Clinical named entity recognition using deep learning models. *AMIA ... Annual Symposium proceedings. AMIA Symposium*, 2017:1812–1819, 04.

Xu, H., Stenner, S. P., Doan, S., Johnson, K. B., Waitman, L. R., and Denny, J. C. (2010). MedEx: a medication information extraction system for clinical narratives. *Journal of the American Medical Informatics Association*, 17:19 – 24.

Zhang, S. and Elhadad, N. (2013). Unsupervised biomedical named entity recognition. *J. of Biomedical Informatics*, 46(6):1088–1098.

Proceedings of MultilingualBIO 2020, pages 15–20
Language Resources and Evaluation Conference (LREC 2020), Marseille, 11–16 May 2020

Localising the Clinical Terminology SNOMED CT by Semi-automated Creation of a German Interface Vocabulary

Stefan Schulz[1,2], Larissa Hammer, David Hashemian-Nik, Markus Kreuzthaler [1]
[1]Institute for Medical Informatics, Statistics and Documentation,
Medical University of Graz, Auenbruggerplatz 2/V, 8036 Graz, Austria,
[2]Averbis GmbH, Salzstraße 15, 79098 Freiburg i.Br., Germany
{stefan.schulz, markus.kreuzthaler}@medunigraz.at

Abstract

Medical language exhibits large variations regarding users, institutions, and language registers. With large parts of clinical information only documented in free text, NLP plays an important role in unlocking potentially re-usable and interoperable meaning from medical records in a multitude of natural languages. This study highlights the role of interface vocabularies. It describes the architectural principles and the evolution of a German interface vocabulary, which is under development by combining machine translation with human annotation and rule-based term generation, yielding a resource with 7.7 million raw entries, each of which linked to the reference terminology SNOMED CT, an international standard with about 350 thousand concepts. The purpose is to offer a high coverage of German medical jargon, in order to optimise terminology grounding of clinical texts by NLP systems. The core resource is a manually maintained table of English-to-German word and chunk translations, supported by a set of language generation rules. We describe a workflow consisting in the enrichment and modification of this table by human and machine efforts, together with top-down and bottom-up methods for terminology population. A term generator generates the final vocabulary by creating one-to-many German variants per SNOMED CT English description. Filtering against a large collection of domain terminologies and corpora drastically reduces the size of the vocabulary in favour of terms that can reasonably be expected to match clinical text passages within a text-mining pipeline. An evaluation was performed by a comparison between the current version of the German interface vocabulary and the English description table of the SNOMED CT International release. An exact term matching was performed with a small parallel corpus constituted by text snippets from different clinical documents. With overall low retrieval parameters (with F-values around 30%), the performance of the German language scenario reaches 80 – 90% of the English one. Interestingly, annotations are slightly better with machine-translated (German – English) texts, using the International SNOMED CT resource only.

Keywords: clinical language, under-resourced languages, technical term generation

1. Introduction

Clinical documentation addresses the needs of health professionals to communicate, collect, and share information for joint decision making, to summarize heterogeneous data, and to customize them to provide optimal support to different use cases.

Electronic health records (EHRs), besides their primary purpose of data presentation and visualisation, bear the potential of large data analysis. It has turned out that structured data do not optimally meet clinicians' documentation and communication requirements, which explains their preference of free text and a general tendency of bias regarding structured (and especially coded) clinical data.

Clinical information ecosystems, their support by computers, and particularly the role clinical language plays therein are far from being ideal. Yet modern clinical care, biomedical research and the translation of the latter into clinical care require ontological and terminological standards in order to make clinical information and data reliable, precise and interoperable.

The need for health data interoperability and exchange is addressed by a multitude of terminology and classification systems, which categorize and define technical terms and their meaning (Schulz et al. 2019; Bodenreider et al., 2018). A certain tragedy lies not only in the fact that these systems interoperate with each other only in exceptional cases and their contents are barely mappable, but also that, despite their commitment to language and concept representation, they are far from representing the jargon that clinicians use in their daily practice. Yet there are some reasons to be optimistic, given the increasing acceptance of large, well-curated terminology systems like SNOMED CT (Millar 2016) and LOINC, used by impressive applications like OHDSI, demonstrating the potential of universal terminologies to integrate and compare data extracts from a variety of clinical information sources (Hripcsak et al., 2018).

Clinical language is largely different from the standard language, including the language used in medical literature. Text is produced in a hurry; often entered directly by clinicians, partly by dictation (with subsequent transcription), increasingly by using speech recognition. Often, no documentation standards are used.

In all these cases, parsimony of expression dominates, to the extent that ambiguous expressions, as long as they are short enough, are preferred, assuming the reader has the context to disambiguate them. Abbreviations and acronyms abound, so that many clinical texts appear overly cryptic even to specialists from other disciplines, let alone to patients. Clinical language is furthermore characterized by incomplete sentences, by lack of grammatical correctness and by a wild mixture of hybrid technical terms that blend the host language with fragments of English, Latin and Greek vocabularies.

The vocabulary mismatch between the clinical jargon and the controlled language of medical terminology systems is immense. For instance, the SNOMED CT concept label "Primary malignant neoplasm of lung" (the eighth most common cause of death worldwide) is unlikely to be literally found in any text written by a doctor. Even in scientific texts (which are of better editorial quality), such artificial terms are highly uncommon. There is no single occurrence of the above term in 27 million MEDLINE records (opposed to about 150,000 hits for the synonym

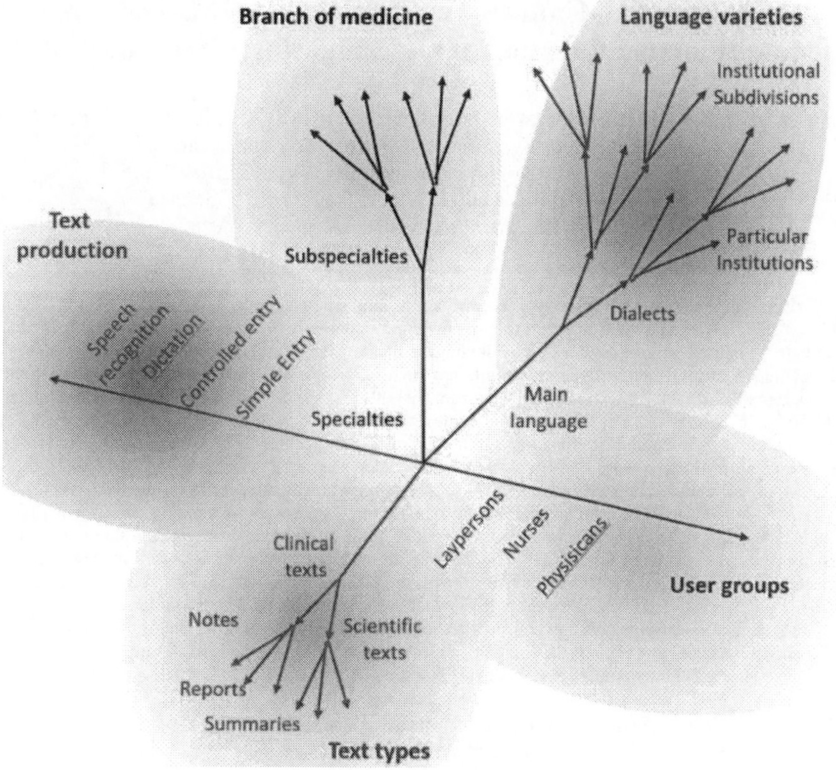

Fig. 1 – Determinants of medical interface terms

"lung cancer"). It is no wonder that terminology implementation studies have shown that standardized terms are often inadequate for clinical use (Højen et al., 2014).
This gap can only be filled by a bottom-up, community-driven non-prescriptive terminology building approach (Schulz et al, 2017). Interface vocabularies, also known as (user) interface terminologies have been proposed (Kalra et al, 2016) as mediators between the real-world clinical language in a given setting (local, national, and user-specific) and international terminology standards like SNOMED CT.
The content of interface vocabularies depends on a series of factors; from language groups (e.g. German, French) to dialects (German spoken in Austria, French spoken in Canada, etc.) to user groups (physicians, nurses, laypersons) to institutions (department A of hospital X, clinic B inside health centre Y) to document types and document sections. The choice of terms also depends on the way the text is produced. Fig. 1 shows how medical language registers are shaped along several axes.
Ideally, an interface vocabulary maps every lexeme into this space, so that most terms become unambiguous according to the context in which they are used. If this context is not known, or not specified in the dictionary, lexical ambiguity becomes a main source of errors in natural language processing.
A manual creation of highly fragmented and specialised interface vocabularies prohibits itself. Instead, automated means should support interface vocabulary creation and management.
There are several use cases for clinical interface vocabularies, some of which are directly related to NLP systems, particularly systems for semantic search within term lists of whole documents, and information extraction. However, collections of interface terms also are important as parts of mono and bilingual dictionaries for specific technical or scientific domains.
Equally important is their use as source for value sets for structured data entry within data acquisition forms, where the terms should be close to the users' language preferences.

2. Materials and Methods

2.1 Source Terminology

SNOMED CT (Millar, 2016) is an ontology-based terminology owned and maintained by the standards development organisation SNOMED International. SNOMED CT is intended to provide the vocabulary needed to represent electronic health records. The current international release has about 350,000 active representational units, called SNOMED concepts. They represent language-independent meanings and are rooted in a formal framework based on the description logics OWL-EL. In this sense, SNOMED CT is very advanced compared to other terminologies. E.g., the concept

Thyroiditis is defined as logically equivalent to a *Disorder* with *Inflammatory morphology* that is located at some *Structure of the thyroid gland*. For several natural languages, SNOMED concepts are linked to one or more technical terms via a so-called description table. E.g., the international English version includes about 950,000 such terms, divided into fully specified terms, i.e. self-explaining, often synthetic labels like the one discussed in the previous section, and synonyms, which are closer to the clinical language in use and correspond to what we have introduced as "interface terms" in section 1. SNOMED CT terms range from single words ("appendectomy", "aspirin") to complex phrases and even sentences ("Computed tomography of neck, chest, abdomen, and pelvis without contrast", "Product containing only sulfamethoxazole and trimethoprim in parenteral dose form").

Besides English, Spanish is the only language for which an official SNOMED CT version, maintained by SNOMED International, exists. Danish and Swedish versions have been locally created, however with only one localised term per concept. For other languages (French, Dutch), partial localization efforts are ongoing. However, for many important languages (German, Italian, Russian, Japanese, Chinese) no SNOMED CT language resources exist, let alone for the multitude of smaller languages, despite their importance in clinical documentation and communication.

2.2 Resources for term harvesting and scoring

Several domain-specific, German language clinical corpora with clinical discharge summaries have been collected at the authors' institution, thanks to several projects on clinical NLP, with authorisation from the institutional ethics committee. In particular, a corpus with about 30,000 cardiology summaries, one with about 5,000 melanoma-related summaries, and one with about 2,000 colorectal cancer summaries were harvested. Another source of clinical language was a database with about 1.7 million unique clinical problem list entries. In addition, the official Austrian drug dictionary was used as a source. For scoring and filtering the machine-generated German interface vocabulary, a collection of 17 German medical terminology systems was exploited, together with a dump from the leading German Medical Journal, the German Wikipedia, filtered by domain, and several drug repositories with drug names, ingredients, and additional drug-related information.

2.3 General Method

A more detailed description of the workflow can be found elsewhere (Hashemian Nik et al., 2019). The main idea of our approach is the combination of machine translation with human translation and validation, as well as a generative process that assembles translations of complete SNOMED CT terms out of their – often highly repetitive – single word or short chunk translations. Briefly, the terminology building process can be described as follows:

Pre-processing

1. Definition of the source terminology (in our case, English textual descriptions (terms) linked to SNOMED CT codes);
2. Identification of terms that are identical across existing translations (e.g. Latin names of organisms);
3. Rule-based chunking of terms into single tokens, noun phrases and prepositional phrases;
4. Sorting chunks and words by decreasing frequency;
5. Submission to neural Web-based translation engines (Google translate, DeepL).

These steps have to be repeated for new terms that come with each semi-annual updates of SNOMED CT.

Specification and implementation

6. Specification of grammar-specific annotations, e.g. POS, gender, number and case for nouns, case for prepositions.
7. Implementation of term building routines, e.g. for adjective / noun inflection and single-word composition, using Python scripts.

Manual curation

8. Manual checking of chunk translation results;
9. Adding new synonyms and spelling variants
10. Adding short forms (acronyms, abbreviations);
11. Identifying ambiguous source terms and adding context-aware translations of longer phrases;

Term creation and manual validation

12. Execution of term assembly routines;
13. Manual assessment of results for formal, stylistic, and content correctness; accordingly repeating former steps, particularly 6, 7, 10, 11.

Bottom-up enhancement by corpora

14. Creation of n-gram lists ("real-world chunks") from clinical corpora, according to the rules developed in 3;
15. Manual mapping of real-world chunks to chunk translation table, iteration of steps 12 and 13.

Validation of progress

16. Validation against benchmarks; blind checking of results against fully machine-translated terms;
17. Manual validation of concept annotations within an NLP pipeline that uses the terminology on real clinical texts.

Enhancement and filtering

18. Exclusion of short (length < 4 characters) acronyms, unless embedded in context (e.g., "CT" is excluded, "CT scan" is preserved).
19. Selection of resources (corpora, dictionaries, databases) to be used as sources of truth for filtering and enhancement;
20. Semi-automated addition of brand names using national drug databases;
21. Creation of rules to harvest spelling variants from external sources (e.g. "ce" vs. "ze", hyphenation vs. spaces or single-word compounds);
22. Defining scoring metrics based on token and n-gram occurrences in external sources;
23. Manual collection of negative examples to constitute patterns for term candidate rejection.

Terminology profiling

24. Using scores and other parameters to filter the terminology according to different usage profiles, e.g. for text mining or value set creation.

2.4 Benchmarking

The interface terminology is periodically checked against a benchmark that was built on top of the results of a multilingual manual SNOMED CT annotation experiment (Miñarro-Gimémez et al., 2018, 2019) for which a small (average 3650 words), but highly diverse corpus had been built, composed by text snippets from clinical documents in six European languages (English, Swedish, French, Dutch, German and Finnish), out of which a parallel corpus was created by medical translators. Texts were annotated with SNOMED CT codes by terminology experts. These texts and related code assignments had never been used in the interface vocabulary building process.

For interface vocabulary benchmarking we re-used the German and English portions of this parallel corpus, together with the SNOMED CT codes attached. For the SNOMED CT representation, two reference standards were used:

- Reference standard R1: annotations using the English, French, Swedish and Dutch versions of SNOMED CT on the respective parallel texts performed by nine terminologists, totalling 2,090 different SNOMED CT codes;
- Reference standard R2: annotation using the English (International) version of SNOMED CT on the English portion of the corpus, performed by two annotators, totalling 1075 different codes (reference standard 2).

These reference standards were used to compare the following scenarios by using a very simple term mapper:

a. SNOMED codes retrieved by matching terms of our German interface vocabulary with the German portion of the corpus;
b. SNOMED codes retrieved by matching English terms of the International SNOMED CT description table[1] with the German portion of the corpus, machine-translated into English by using the freely available Google translator;
c. SNOMED codes retrieved by matching English terms of the International SNOMED CT description table[1] with the English portion of the corpus.

The concept mapper is based on exact match between one or more decapitalised tokens, iterating over the vocabulary reversely ordered by string length. For each match of a lexicon entry the corresponding string is removed from the corpus and the SNOMED CT code(s) assigned to it is (are) stored. The resulting code sets are compared to the set of codes in R1 and R2; and precision, recall and F-measures are calculated.

3. Results

The work started in 2014 with limited resources (one part-time terminologist and one to three medical students working on average 8 hours per week). Since then, it has been subject to constant optimization and quality improvement.

The current size of the terminology is about 7.7 million records, each record consisting of the SNOMED identifier, an interface term ID, the English source term and the automatically generated German interface term. Table 1 shows an example of eight German interface terms, automatically created out of two English SNOMED terms. All eight translations are correct in content and understandable, but only those in bold are grammatically correct and likely to be found in clinical documents. The interface terms were generated out of 125 thousand German word / chunk translations from about 100,000 English words / chunks.

An analysis of the current quality of the interface terminology by blinded human assessment terminology stated equivalence regarding content correctness when comparing a random interface term with the (only) term that resulted from the machine translation system DeepL (Hashemian Nik et al., 2019). However, the results show deficits regarding grammar, spelling, and style issues of the current state of the interface vocabulary. The same study revealed that a case insensitive, spelling variation tolerant match between an ideal translation suggested by a domain expert (not knowing the generated results) occurred with half of the machine-generated interface terms.

The combinatory explosion observed especially with long SNOMED term translations, many of which are not ideal and some of them not even understandable makes filtering and profiling necessary.

Code	English	German
53701004	Sebaceous gland activity	Glandula sebacea Tätigkeit
		Glandula sebacea Aktivität
		Talgdrüsentätigkeit
		Talgdrüsenaktivität
	Sebaceous gland secretion	Glandula sebacea Absonderung
		Glandula sebacea Sekretion
		Talgdrüsenabsonderung
		Talgdrüsensekretion

Table 1: Example of a SNOMED CT code, two English terms and eight generated German terms

We started with three profiles, viz. (i) one for text mining, limited to terms with a maximum of six tokens; another one (ii) in which only terms that literally matched the resources (cf. subsection 1.2) were preserved; and a third one (iii) which allowed more flexibility regarding plausibility checking, and in which up to 50 synonyms above a quality threshold were accepted.
Whereas (i) yielded 506 thousand interface terms (6.5% of the raw list), (ii) yielded only 89 thousand (1.2%), and (iii) 387 thousand. The corresponding coverage of SNOMED CT codes was 39% for (i), 17% for (ii) and 29% for (iii).

[1] which includes canonical and interface terms

The rationale for producing different profiles is explained by the use cases to be served by the interface vocabulary. For text mining purposes, exact or moderately fuzzy matches of terms with more than six tokens are very unlikely. On the other hand, implausible terms (because of combinations), which hardly ever match are harmless.

In cases where interface terms are created for human use (e.g. supporting picklists or auto-completion functionality for data entry), well-formedness, comprehensibility and currency are crucial. However, by using a strict filter, many of the synthetically created labels, like the above-discussed "primary malignant neoplasm of the lung" would be thrown out, because they do not occur in medical documents and not even in other terminology sources. The benchmark results are given in Table 2 and Table 3.

Experiment R1	Precision	Recall	F_1
a. German texts	0.49	0.16	0.28
b. German texts, machine translated	0.48	0.16	0.28
c. English texts	0.50	0.19	0.31

Table 2: Retrieval performance using reference standard R1 (pooled annotations by nine terminology experts, performed with English, Swedish, Dutch, and French SNOMED CT translations, performed on the respective language portion of the ASSESS-CT parallel corpus).

Experiment R2	Precision	Recall	F_1
a. German texts	0.36	0.23	0.29
b. German texts, machine translated	0.37	0.25	0.30
c. English texts	0.41	0.31	0.35

Table 3: Retrieval performance using reference standard R2 (pooled annotations by two terminology experts, performed with the SNOMED CT version on the English language portion of the ASSESS-CT parallel corpus).

4. Discussion and Outlook

We have outlined a complex heuristics that generates German interface terms for SNOMED CT concepts. In a previous work, we had demonstrated that its quality was roughly comparable to fully machine-generated terms. The advantage of our approach however was the high term productivity compared with machine translation, especially the assembly of term variants that are rare but useful, especially for data entry and text mining. A natural next step would be to exploit neural term harvesting approaches for additional terminology enrichment. Word embeddings might help retrieve new synonyms, but they also will require large amounts of training resources, which are difficult to acquire in a clinical context, let alone sharable among researchers.

Another strand of future work is the increased incorporation of acronyms and other short forms into the resource. So far, we have re-used existing acronym lists and have manually expanded acronyms from our clinical sources, but the ambiguity of two and three character acronyms is high. This is the reason why single acronyms with four characters and are suppressed in our pipeline, whereas longer terms containing them are released, e.g. "DM type 1" where sense disambiguation can be expected from the local context.

The benchmarking results provide interesting insights in the problems around terminology grounding of clinical texts, the peculiarities of a huge terminology like SNOMED CT, about the current quality of the German interface terminology and finally about the raison d'être of terminology translations in general.

It must be emphasised that the results given in tables 2 and 3 were not the result of text analysis in a NLP pipeline (for which better results should be expected, but of an overly simple term matching algorithm). The problem of finding the right SNOMED CT code for a passage of clinical text – even by terminology experts – was described in depth by Miñarro-Giménez et al. (2018, 2019), who reported an astonishingly low inter-annotator agreement of about 40% (Krippendorff's α). That a team of nine annotators had come up with more than double the numbers of codes for the same content (in four languages), compared to a pair of coders (for English only) sheds light on the high degree of personal discretion involved. Of course, this meant that for many chunks of clinical meaning there were many annotations with semantically closely related codes, which explains the overall low recall, especially in the R1 scenario. The expert annotation task had also privileged SNOMED pre-co-ordinations, e.g. for "Fracture of the neck of the femur", which did not match expressions in the text like "The neck of the left femur was broken". Our term matching text might have matched the single codes "neck", "femur", "left", and "broken". However, this phenomenon is expected in all scenarios. Another characteristic of the corpus, which explains low performance values, is the frequency of acronyms and other short forms, e.g. the roman numbers "I" to "XII" for the cranial nerves.

Coming back to the primary purpose of this benchmarking, viz. the comparison of the German interface vocabulary created by the authors with the nearly one-million English term list that comes with the International SNOMED CT release (and which includes many close-to-user terms), the figures are remarkable insofar the performance of the German language scenario reaches 80 to 90% of the performance of the English one.

Finally, the figures on the alternative strategy, viz. machine-translating non-English clinical texts to English with Google Translate and checking against the original English SNOMED CT term list, could be a starting point for a radical re-thinking of multilingual text processing. Is it still worthwhile developing multilingual resources if neural machine translation (even not trained with specific clinical text) yields increasingly better results? Concentrating human efforts on improving the already very rich inventory of tools and resources for English could then be a better idea than creating and maintaining language resources for a multitude of different languages with insufficient financial and human resources.

Current versions of the resource can be downloaded from http://user.medunigraz.at/stefan.schulz/mugit/

5. Acknowledgements

This work was partly supported by the EU projects SEMCARE – 7th FP grant 611388; ASSESS-CT - H2020-PHC-2014-15, grant 643818.

6. Bibliographical References

Bodenreider, O., Cornet, R., Vreeman, D.J. (2018). Recent Developments in Clinical Terminologies - SNOMED CT, LOINC, and RxNorm. *Yearb Med Inform*, 27(1):129-139.

Hashemian Nik, D., Kasáč, Z., Goda, Z., Semlitsch, A., Schulz, S. (2019). Building an Experimental German User Interface Terminology Linked to SNOMED CT. *Stud Health Technol Inform*, 264:153-157.

Højen, A.R., Elberg, P.B., Andersen, S.K. (2014). SNOMED CT adoption in Denmark - why is it so hard? *Stud Health Technol Inform.* 205:226-230.

Hripcsak, G., Levine, M.E., Shang, N., Ryan, P.B. (2018). Effect of vocabulary mapping for conditions on phenotype cohorts. *JAMIA*, 25(12):1618-1625.

Kalra, D., Schulz, S., Karlsson, D., Vander Stichele, R., Cornet, R., Rosenbeck Gøeg, K., Cangioli, G., Chronaki, C., Thiel, R., Thun, S., Stroetmann, V. (2016). *Assessing SNOMED CT for Large Scale eHealth Deployments in the EU. ASSESS CT Recommendations.* http://assess-ct.eu/final-brochure.html.

Millar J.(2016). The Need for a Global Language - SNOMED CT Introduction. *Stud Health Technol Inform*, 225:683-685.

Miñarro-Giménez, J.A., Cornet, R., Jaulent, M.C., Dewenter, H., Thun, S., Gøeg, K.R., Karlsson, D., Schulz, S. (2019) Quantitative analysis of manual annotation of clinical text samples. *Int J Med Inform.*:123:37-48

Miñarro-Giménez, J.A., Martínez-Costa, C., Karlsson, D., Schulz, S., Gøeg, K.R. (2018). Qualitative analysis of manual annotations of clinical text with SNOMED CT. *PLoS One.* Dec 27:3(12)

Schulz, S., Daumke, P., Romacker, M., López-García, P. (2019). Representing oncology in datasets: Standard or custom biomedical terminology? *Informatics in Medicine Unlocked*, 15:100186.

Schulz, S., Rodrigues, J.M., Rector, A., Chute, C.G. (2017). Interface Terminologies, Reference Terminologies and Aggregation Terminologies: A Strategy for Better Integration. *Stud Health Technol Inform*, 245:940-944.

Proceedings of MultilingualBIO 2020, pages 21–28
Language Resources and Evaluation Conference (LREC 2020), Marseille, 11–16 May 2020

Multilingual enrichment of disease biomedical ontologies

Léo Bouscarrat[1,2], Antoine Bonnefoy[1], Cécile Capponi[2], Carlos Ramisch[2]
[1]EURA NOVA, Marseille, France
[2]Aix Marseille Univ, Université de Toulon, CNRS, LIS, Marseille, France
{leo.bouscarrat, antoine.bonnefoy}@euranova.eu
{leo.bouscarrat, cecile.capponi, carlos.ramisch}@lis-lab.fr

Abstract

Translating biomedical ontologies is an important challenge, but doing it manually requires much time and money. We study the possibility to use open-source knowledge bases to translate biomedical ontologies. We focus on two aspects: coverage and quality. We look at the coverage of two biomedical ontologies focusing on diseases with respect to Wikidata for 9 European languages (Czech, Dutch, English, French, German, Italian, Polish, Portuguese and Spanish) for both ontologies, plus Arabic, Chinese and Russian for the second one. We first use direct links between Wikidata and the studied ontologies and then use second-order links by going through other intermediate ontologies. We then compare the quality of the translations obtained thanks to Wikidata with a commercial machine translation tool, here Google Cloud Translation.

Keywords: biomedical, ontology, translation, wikidata

1. Introduction

Biomedical ontologies, like Orphanet (INSERM, 1999b), play an important role in many downstream tasks (Andronis et al., 2011; Li et al., 2015; Phan et al., 2017), especially in natural language processing (Maldonado et al., 2017; Nayel and Shashrekha, 2019). Today either the vast majority of these ontologies are only available in English or their restrictive licenses reduce the scope of their usage. There is nowadays a real focus on reducing the prominence of English, thus on working on less-resourced languages. To do so, there is a need for resources in other languages, but the creation of such resources is time and money consuming.

At the same time, the Internet is also a source of incredible projects aiming to gather a maximum of knowledge in a maximum of languages. One of them is the collaborative encyclopedia Wikipedia, opened in 2001, which currently exists in more than 300 languages. As it contains mainly plain text, it is hard to use it as a resource as is. However, several knowledge bases have been built from it: DBpedia (Lehmann et al., 2015) and Wikidata (Vrandečić and Krötzsch, 2014). The main difference between these two knowledge graphs is the update process: while Wikidata is manually updated by users, DBpedia extracts its information directly from Wikipedia. Compared to biomedical ontologies they are structured using less expressive formalisms and they gather information about a larger domain. They are open-source, thus can be used for any downstream tasks. For each entity they have a preferred label, but sometimes also alternative labels that can be used as synonyms. For example, the entity *Q574227* in Wikidata has the preferred label *2q37 monosomy* in English along with the alternative labels in English: *Albright Hereditary Osteodystrophy-Like Syndrome* and *Brachydactyly Mental Retardation Syndrome*. Moreover, entities in these two knowledge bases also have translations in several languages. For example, the entity *Q574227* in Wikidata has the preferred label *2q37 monosomy* in English and the preferred label *Zespół delecji 2q37* in Polish. They also feature some links between their own entities and entities in external biomedical ontologies. For example, the entity *Q574227* in Wikidata has a property *Orphanet ID* (*P1550*) with the value *1001*.

By using both kinds of resources, biomedical ontologies and open-source knowledge bases, we could partially enrich biomedical ontologies in languages other than English. As links between the entities of these resources are already existing, we expect good quality. To further enrich them we could even look at second-order links since many biomedical ontologies also contain some links to other ontologies.

The goal of this work is twofold:

- to study the coverage of such open-source collaborative knowledge graphs compared to biomedical ontologies,
- to study the quality of the translations using first- and second-order links and comparing this quality with the quality obtained by machine translation tools.

This paper is part of a long-term project whose goal is to work on multilingual disease extraction from news with strategies based on dictionary expansion. Consequently, we need a multilingual vocabulary with diseases which are normalized with respect to an ontology. Thus, we focus on one kind of biomedical ontologies, that is, ontologies about diseases.

2. Resources and Related Work

There has already been some work trying to use open-source knowledge bases to translate biomedical ontologies. Bretschneider et al. (2014) obtain a German-English medical dictionary using DBPedia. The goal is to perform information extraction from a German biomedical corpus. They could not directly use the RadLex ontology (Langlotz, 2006) as it is only available in English. So, they first extract term candidates in their German corpus. Then, they try to match the candidates with the pairs in their German-English dictionary. If a candidate is in the dictionary, they

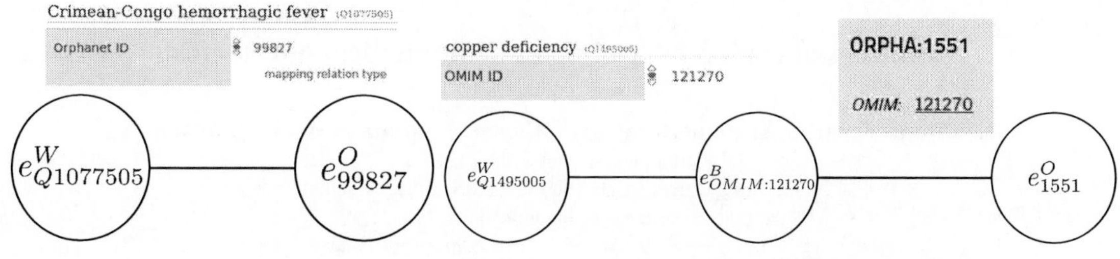

Figure 1: Example of first-order link (left) and second-order link (right)

use the translation to match with the RadLex ontology. Finally, this term candidate alongside with the match in the RadLex ontology is processed by a human to validate the matching.

Alba et al. (2017) create a language-independent method to maintain up-to-date ontologies by extracting new instances from text. This method is based on a human-in-the-loop who helps tuning scores and thresholds for the extraction. Their method requires some "contexts" to start finding new entities to add to the ontology. To bootstrap the contexts, they can either ask a human to annotate some data or use an oracle made by the dictionary extracted from the DBpedia and Wikidata using word matching on the corpus. They then look for good candidates, i.e., a set of words surrounding an item, by looking for elements in similar contexts to the one found using the bootstrapping. Then, a human-in-the-loop validates the newly found entities, adding them to the dictionary if they are correct, or down-voting the context if they are not relevant entities.

Hailu et al. (2014) work on the translation of the Gene Ontology from English to German and compare three different approaches: DBpedia, the Google Translate API without context, and the Google Translate API with context. To find the terms in DBpedia they use keyword-based search. After a human evaluation, they find that translations obtained with DBpedia have the lowest coverage (only 25%) and quality compared to those obtained with Google Translate API. However, to compare the quality of the different methods they only use the translation of 75 terms obtained with DBpedia compared to 1,000 with Google Translate API. They also note that synonyms could be a useful tool for machine translation and that using keyword-based exact match query to match the two sources could explain the low coverage.

Silva et al. (2015) compare three methods to translate SNOMED CT from English to Portuguese: DBpedia, ICD-9 and Google Translate. To verify the quality of the different approaches they use the CPARA ontology which has been hand-mapped to SNOMED CT. It is composed of 191 terms and focused on allergies and adverse reactions. They detect coverage of 10% with the ICD-9, 37% with DBpedia and 100% with Google Translate. To compare the quality of their translations they use the Jaro Similarity (Jaro, 1989).

We elaborate on these ideas by adding some elements. First of all, compared to Hailu et al. (2014) and Silva et al. (2015), we use already existing properties to perform the matching between the biomedical ontology and the knowledge graph, which should improve the quality with regard to the previous works. We also go further than these first-order links and explore the possibility of using second-order links to improve the coverage of the mappings between the sources. Compared to the same works, we also present a more complete study, Hailu et al. (2014) only evaluate on 75 terms and Silva et al. (2015) on 191 terms. We compare the coverage and quality of the entire biomedical ontology containing 10,444 terms. Furthermore, as we want to use the result of this work for biomedical entity recognition, synonyms of entities are really important for recall and also for normalisation, thus we also quantify the difference of quantity of synonyms between the original biomedical ontology and those found with Wikidata.

In this work, as we focus on diseases, we use a free dataset extracted from Orphanet (INSERM, 1999b) to perform the evaluation. Orphanet is a resource built to gather and improve knowledge about rare diseases. Through Orphadata (INSERM, 1999a), free datasets of aggregated data are updated monthly. One of them is about rare diseases, including cross-references to other ontologies. The Orphadata dataset contains the translation of 10,444 entities for English, French, German, Spanish, Dutch, Italian, Portuguese, 10,418 entities in Polish and 9,323 in Czech. All the translations have been validated by experts, thus can be used as a gold standard for multilingual ontology enrichment. One issue of this dataset is that rare diseases are, by definition, not well known. Therefore, one may expect a lower coverage than a less focused dataset; thus we propose to also measure the coverage of another dataset, Disease Ontology (Schriml et al., 2019). However we cannot use it to evaluate the translation task as it does not contain translations.

As an external knowledge base, we use Wikidata. It has many links to external ontologies, especially links to biomedical ontologies such as *wdt:P1550* for Orphanet, *wdt:P699* for Disease Ontology, and *wdt:P492* for the Online Mendelian Inheritance in Man (OMIM). It is also important to note that, over the 9 languages we studied, only the Czech Wikipedia has less than 1,000,000 articles. This information can be used as a proxy for the completeness of the information in each language on Wikidata. We prefer it over DBpedia as we find it easier to use, especially to find the properties.

As a machine translation tool, we use Google Cloud Translation. It is a paying service offered by Google Cloud.

3. Methods and Experiments

In this section, we first define the notations used in this paper, then we describe how we extract the first- and second-order links from our sources. Afterwards, we describe how we perform machine translation. The evaluation metrics are subsequently explained and finally we describe our evaluation protocol.

3.1. Definition and Notations

We define:

- e_i^S as an entity in the source knowledge base S, $S \in [O, W, B]$ where O is Orphanet, W is WikiData and B are all the other external biomedical ontologies used. An entity is either a concept in an ontology or in a knowledge graph.

- $E^S = \{e_i^S\}_{i=1...|E^S|}$ is the set of all the entities in the source S.

- $E = E^O \cup E^W \cup E^B$ is the set of all the entities in all the sources.

- $\mathrm{L}_l(e)$ is the preferred label of the entity e in the language l, or $\emptyset$ if there is no label in this language.

- $\mathcal{L}_l(e)$ represents all the possible labels of the entity e in the language l or $\emptyset$ if there is no label in this language. Furthermore, $\mathrm{L}_l(e) \in \mathcal{L}_l(e)$

- T is a set of links, such that $t \in T$ with $t = (e_i^s, e_j^{s'}), s \neq s'$.

- $G = (E, T)$ is an undirected graph.

- $\mathcal{V}(e_i) = \{e_j \in E | \exists t \in T, t = (e_i, e_j)\}$, defines the set of all the neighbours of the entity e_i.

- $\mathcal{W}(e) = \{v \in \mathcal{V}(e) | v \in W\}$, defines the set of all the neighbours that are in Wikidata of the entity e.

- $MT(\{s_1, ..., s_n\}, l)$ is a function that returns the labels $\{s_1, ..., s_n\}$ translated from English to the language l thanks to Google Cloud Translation.

3.2. Gathering Links between Entities

3.2.1. First-Order Links

The first step of our method consists in gathering all the information about the sources. To obtain the gold translations, we use Orphadata. We collected all the JSON files from their website[1] on January 15, 2020. We extract the OrphaNumber, the Name, the SynonymList and the ExternalReferenceList of each element in the files.

For WikiData we use the SPARQL endpoint[2]. We query all the entities having a property OrphaNumber *wdt:P1550*, and, for these entities, we obtain all their preferred labels (*rdfs:label*) and synonyms (*skos:altLabel*), corresponding to E_i^O in the 9 European languages included in Orphanet. The base aggregator of the synonyms uses a comma to separate them. In our case, this error-prone because the comma can also be part of the label, for example one of the alternative label of the entity *Q55786560* is *49, XXXYY syndrome*. We needed to concatenate the synonyms with another symbol[3]. Thanks to the property which gives the Orphanumber of the related entity in Orphanet we can create links $t = (e^O, e^W)$ between an entity e_i^W in Wikidata and and entity e_i^O in Orphanet.

The mapping is then trivial, as we have the OrphaNumber in the two sources. On the left of Figure 1 we can see that the entity *Q1077505* in Wikidata has a property *Orphanet ID* with the value *99827*, thus we can create $t = (Q1077505^W, 99827^O)$. Nonetheless, the mapping is not always unary, because several Wikidata entities can be linked to the same Orphanet entity.

Formally, the set of Orphanet entities with at least one first-order link is:

$$E^F = \{e \in E^O | \exists w \in W, (e, w) \in T\}$$

3.2.2. Second-Order Links

Orphanet provides some external references to auxiliary ontologies. We add these references to our graph: $t = (e^O, e^B) \in T$. Even if there are already first-order links between Orphanet and Wikidata, we cannot ensure that all the entities are linked. To improve the coverage of translations, we can use second-order links, creating an indirect link when entities from Wikidata and Orphanet are linked to the same entity in a third external source B. For example, on the right of Figure 1, we extract the link between the entity *Q1495005* of Wikidata and the entity *121270* of OMIM. We also extract from Orphanet that the entity *1551* of Orphanet is link to the same entity of OMIM. Therefore, as a second-order relation, the entity *Q1495005* of Wikidata and the entity *1551* of Orphanet are linked.

The objective is to find some links $t' = (e^W, e^B)$ where $\exists v \in \mathcal{V}(e^B)$ and $v \in E^O$. Consequently, we are looking for links between entities from Wikidata and the external biomedical ontologies, whenever the entity in the external biomedical ontology already has a link with an entity in Orphanet.

For that purpose, we extract all the links between Wikidata and the external biomedical ontologies in the same fashion as from Orphanet, using the appropriate Wikidata properties. In the previous example, we create links $(Q1495005^W, OMIM : 121270^B) \in T$ and $(1551^O, OMIM : 121270^B) \in T$.

[1] `http://www.orphadata.org/cgi-bin/rare_free.html`

[2] `https://query.wikidata.org/sparql` can be queried with the interface `https://query.wikidata.org/`

[3] We made a package to extract entities from Wikidata: `https://github.com/euranova/wikidata_property_extraction`

We can now map Wikidata and Orphanet using second-order links. This set of links is denoted as:

$$C = \{e \in E^O | \exists (w, b) \in E^W \times E^B, \\ (e, b) \in T, (w, b) \in T\}$$

We also define the set of all the second-order linked Wikipedia entities of a specific Orphanet entity:

$$\mathcal{C}(e^O) = \{w \in E^W | \exists b \in E^B, (e, b) \in T, (w, b) \in T\}$$

3.3. Machine Translation

We use Google Cloud Translation as a machine translation tool to translate the labels of the ontology from English to a target language. As we want to have the same entities in the test set as for Wikidata, for each language we only translate the Orphanet entities which have at least one first-order link to an entity in Wikidata with a label in the target language. So for an entity e, for the language l the output of Google Cloud Translation is:

$$MT(\mathcal{L}_{en}(e), l)$$

3.4. Definition of Evaluation Metrics

In this section, we define the different evaluation metrics that are used to evaluate the efficiency of the method.

3.4.1. Coverage Metric

To estimate the coverage of Wikipedia on a biomedical ontology we use the following metric:

$$Coverage(E_1, E_2, l) = \frac{|\{e \in E_1 | \mathrm{L}_l(e) \neq \emptyset\}|}{|\{e' \in E_2 | \mathrm{L}_l(e') \neq \emptyset\}|}$$

where E_1 and E_2 are sets of entities.

3.4.2. Jaro Similarity and n-ary Jaro

In order to evaluate the quality of the translations, we follow Silva et al. (2015) choosing the Jaro similarity, which is a type of edit distance. We made this choice as we are looking at entities. Whereas other measures such as BLEU (Papineni et al., 2002) are widely used for translation tasks, they have been designed for full sentences instead of relatively short ontology labels. The Jaro Similarity is defined as:

$$\mathrm{J}(s, s') = \frac{1}{3}\left(\frac{m}{|\, s\,|} + \frac{m}{|\, s'\,|} + \frac{m-t}{m}\right) s, s' \in \{a, ..., z\}^*$$

with s and s' two strings, $|\ s\ |$ the length of s, t is half the number of transpositions, m the number of *matching characters*. Two characters from s and s' are *matching* if they are the same and not further than $\frac{max(|s|,|s'|)}{2} - 1$. The Jaro Similarity ranges between 0 and 1, where the score is 1 when the two strings are the same.

However, since one Orphanet entity may have several neighbour Wikidata entities, we cannot use the Jaro similarity directly. We choose to use the max, for considering the quality of the closest entity:

$$\mathcal{J}_{\max}(s, [s_1, ..., s_n]) = \max_{s' \in [s_1, ..., s_n]} \mathrm{J}(s, s')$$

3.4.3. Quality Metrics

From assessing the quality of the translations, we create 4 different measures with different goals. For each entity in each language, there is a preferred label $\mathrm{L}_l(e)$ and a list of all the possible labels $\mathcal{L}_l(e)$. All of the metrics range between 0 and 1, the higher the better.

$$\mathcal{M}_{\mathrm{p}}\mathrm{l}\,(e, [e_1, ..., e_n], l) = \mathcal{J}_{\max}\left(\mathrm{L}_l(e), [\mathrm{L}_l(e_1), .., \mathrm{L}_l(e_n)]\right)$$

$$\mathcal{M}_{\mathrm{b}}\mathrm{l}\,(e, [e_1, ..., e_n], l) = \mathcal{J}_{\max}\left(\mathrm{L}_l(e), \bigcup_{i=1}^{n} \mathcal{L}_l(e_i)\right)$$

$$\mathcal{M}_{\mathrm{m}}\mathrm{bl}\,(e, [e_1, ..., e_n], l) = \underset{s \in \mathcal{L}_l(e)}{mean}\ \mathcal{J}_{\max}\left(s, \bigcup_{i=1}^{n} \mathcal{L}_l(e_i)\right)$$

$$\mathcal{M}_{\mathrm{M}}\mathrm{bl}\,(e, [e_1, ..., e_n], l) = \max_{s \in \mathcal{L}_l(e)} \mathcal{J}_{\max}\left(s, \bigcup_{i=1}^{n} \mathcal{L}_l(e_i)\right)$$

$\mathcal{M}_{\mathrm{p}}\mathrm{l}$, for principal label, compares the preferred labels from Orphanet and Wikidata. This number is expected to be high, but as there is no reason that Wikidata and Orphanet use the same preferred label, we do not expect it to be the highest score. Nonetheless, as Wikidata is a collaborative platform, a score of 1 on a high number of entities in a different language could also indicate that the translations come from Orphanet.

$\mathcal{M}_{\mathrm{b}}\mathrm{l}$, for best label, compares the preferred label from Orphanet against all the labels in Wikidata. The goal here is to verify that the preferred label of Orphanet is available in Wikidata.

$\mathcal{M}_{\mathrm{m}}\mathrm{bl}$, for mean best label, takes the average of the similarity of one label in Orphanet against all the labels in Wikidata. This score can be seen as a completeness score, it evaluates the ability of finding all the labels of Orphanet in Wikidata.

$\mathcal{M}_{\mathrm{M}}\mathrm{bl}$, for max best label, takes the maximum of the similarity of one label in Orphanet against all the labels in Wikidata. The question behind this metric is: Do we have at least one label in common between Orphanet and Wikidata? A low score here could mean that the relation is erroneous. We expect a score close to 1 here.

We used the same measures for the machine-translated dataset, however, the difference between $\mathcal{M}_{\mathrm{p}}\mathrm{l}$ and $\mathcal{M}_{\mathrm{b}}\mathrm{l}$ is expected to be smaller, as we are sure that the preferred label from the translated dataset is the translation of the preferred label from Orphanet.

To obtain a score for these measures on the entire dataset, we compute the average of the scores over all Orphanet entities.

3.5. Protocol

The first step of our experiments is the extraction of first-order and second-order links from Wikidata and Orphanet as explained in 3.2.. Once these links are available, we study them, starting with their coverage. To evaluate

	$\mathcal{M}_p$l			$\mathcal{M}_b$l			$\mathcal{M}_m$bl			$\mathcal{M}_M$bl		
Lang	1st W	1+2nd W	GCT	1st W	1+2nd W	GCT	1st W	1+2nd W	GCT	1st W	1+2nd W	GCT
EN	85.5	**87.5**	N/A	91.5	**92.1**	N/A	**84.1**	80.5	N/A	**97.3**	96.6	N/A
FR	85.3	82.4	**89.8**	87.4	84.2	**90.5**	75.7	69.3	**90.1**	94.1	89.1	**97.7**
DE	77.1	67.8	**80.5**	79.1	70.3	**81.6**	67.5	60.9	**83.4**	88.7	79.0	**95.4**
ES	81.3	70.1	**92.5**	84.4	73.0	**93.0**	68.7	58.4	**90.2**	91.7	89.1	**98.3**
PL	78.0	63.8	**82.0**	82.0	61.3	**83.2**	66.6	55.9	**85.0**	90.7	77.3	**95.7**
IT	79.4	66.7	**88.4**	82.4	68.8	**89.5**	69.1	58.5	**88.1**	90.5	77.4	**97.2**
PT	79.9	64.9	**83.6**	82.1	66.5	**87.6**	**73.7**	60.8	68.4	93.5	83.5	**93.3**
NL	72.9	59.1	**88.0**	75.6	60.9	**88.7**	65.8	55.1	**89.9**	86.5	71.4	**97.2**
CS	76.3	52.8	**81.9**	79.1	54.9	**83.3**	67.5	52.3	**85.4**	88.7	68.8	**95.3**

Table 1: Scores of the different methods with the different metrics in function of the languages. 1st W represents the quality of the first-order links with Wikidata, 1+2nd W the first and second-order links, and GCT the translations obtained by Google Cloud Translation.

the coverage of Wikidata for each language, we compute $Coverage(E^F, E^O, l)$ for the 9 languages. We also compute $Coverage(C, E^O, l)$ for second-order links. As Orphanet is focused on rare diseases, we do not expect a high coverage in Wikidata. To verify this hypothesis, we do the same evaluation on the Disease Ontology, which does not focus on rare diseases.
Then, we study the quality of the different methods. We apply the 4 quality metrics defined in 3.4.3. for each language on each method:

- First-order links: $\underset{e^O \in E^F}{mean}(\mathcal{M}(e^O, \mathcal{W}(e^O)), l)$
- Second-order links: $\underset{e^O \in C}{mean}(\mathcal{M}(e^O, \mathcal{C}(e^O), l)$
- Machine translation: $\underset{e^O \in E^F}{mean}(\mathcal{M}(e^O, MT(\mathcal{L}_{e^O}(l), l), l)$

Finally, we look at the number of labels we can obtain for both sources.

- Orphanet: $\underset{e \in E^F}{mean}|\mathcal{L}_l(e)|$
- Wikidata: $\underset{e \in E^F}{mean} \sum_{w \in \mathcal{W}(e)} |\mathcal{L}_l(w)|$
- GCT: $\underset{e \in E^F}{mean}|MT(\mathcal{L}_{en}(e), l)|$

The number of synonyms of an entity e in a language l is: $|\mathcal{L}_l(e)|$, and we also remove the duplicates. We then average this over all the entities which are in a first-order link and in Wikidata and Orphanet.

4. Results

In this part, we first present the results on the coverage of Wikipedia on Orphanet, then we present the quality of the translation. Afterwards, we show results about the number of synonyms in both sources and finally we discuss these results.[4]

4.1. Coverage

4.1.1. Orphanet

First, we evaluate the coverage for each language, i.e., the percentage of entities in Orphanet which have at least one translation in Wikidata.
The Orphadata dataset contains translations of English, French, German, Spanish, Dutch, Italian, Portuguese, Polish and Czech. For Wikidata, the results depend on the language as not all the entities have translations in every language.

Language	Orphanet	Wikidata (%)
English	10,444	8,870 (84.9%)
French	10,444	5,038 (48.2%)
German	10,444	1,946 (18.6%)
Spanish	10,444	1,565 (15.0%)
Polish	10,171	1,329 (13.1%)
Italian	10,444	1,175 (11.3%)
Portuguese	10,444	921 (8.8%)
Dutch	10,444	888 (8.5%)
Czech	9,323	452 (4.8%)

Table 2: Number of translated entities in Orphanet and number of Orphanet entities having at least one translation in Wikidata with first-order links. The percentage of coverage is shown in parentheses.

As we can see in Table 2 that coverage depends on the language. The coverage of English gives us the amount of entities from Orphanet having at least one link with Wikidata. Here, we have 84.9% of the entities which are already linked to at least one entity in Wikidata. It means that the property of the OrphaNumber is widely used. We can also note that the French Wikidata seems to carry more information about rare diseases than the German Wikipedia. Indeed French and German Wikipedias have approximately the same global size[5], but the German Wikidata contains much less information about rare diseases.

[4]The results can be reproduced with this code: `https://github.com/euranova/orphanet_translation`

[5]As of the 6th February 2020: `https://meta.wikimedia.org/wiki/List_of_Wikipedias`

Language	Cov 1st (%)	Cov 1st+2nd (%)
English	8,870 (84.9%)	9,317 (89.2%)
French	5,038 (48.2%)	7,922 (75.9%)
German	1,946 (18.6%)	6,350 (60.8%)
Spanish	1,565 (15.0%)	6,122 (58.6%)
Polish	1,329 (13.1%)	5,797 (57.0%)
Italian	1,175 (11.3%)	5,715 (54.7%)
Portuguese	921 (8.8%)	5,016 (48.0%)
Dutch	888 (8.5%)	5,081 (48.6%)
Czech	452 (4.8%)	3,180 (34.1%)

Table 3: Coverage in terms of number and percentage of entities in Wikidata linked to Orphanet using first-order links (Cov 1st) and first- plus second-order links (Cov 1st+2nd).

The next question is the quantity of new links we can obtain by gathering second-order links.
Table 3 shows that the second-order links improve the coverage. For English, the improvement is small. Thus, for all the other languages, second-order links really help to increase the coverage. It seems to be a good help for average-resourced languages. We have used ICD-10, Medical Subject Heading (MeSH), Online Mendelian Inheritance in Man (OMIM), and, Unified Medical Language System (UMLS) as auxiliary ontologies.

4.1.2. Disease Ontology

Even if the coverage for Orphanet in English is already high, Orphanet is focused on rare diseases, which is really specific. This specificity could have an impact on the coverage as Wikidata is not made by experts. To verify if the specificity of this ontology has an influence on coverage, we have also looked at another biomedical ontology on diseases, Disease Ontology. It is also about diseases but does not focus on rare disease. Thus, this difference in generality is expected to have an impact on the coverage.
The Disease Ontology contains 12,171 concepts. We plan to use it for future works on other languages: Arabic, Russian and Chinese. These three languages also have Wikipedias with more than 1,000,000 articles on which we could rely.
As expected, this less expert ontology seems to have better coverage than Orphanet. Table 4 shows that, even if the coverage for all the languages is better than for Orphanet, the difference is not the same for all the languages. Especially, Spanish has a coverage in Disease Ontology superior to that in Orphadata by more than 11%. We do not have an explanation for these differences.
We do not compute the second-order links for Disease Ontology because 97.2% of the Orphanet entities are already linked using first-order links.

4.2. Quality

The next question concerns the quality of the translations obtained. We can expect high-quality translations from Google Cloud Translation, but to what extent? We also want to compare the quality of translations obtained from Wikidata using first-order and second-order links. The ontology we use is heavily linked directly to Wikidata, but this is not the case for all the ontologies. For ontologies with lower first-order coverage, one could expect higher increase of the second-order coverage as observed in Table 3.

Language	Wikidata (%)
English	11,833 (97.2%)
French	7,156 (58.8%)
Spanish	3,178 (26.1%)
Arabic	2,507 (20.6%)
German	2,500 (20.5%)
Italian	2,098 (17.2%)
Polish	1,869 (15.3%)
Chinese	1,789 (14.7%)
Portuguese	1,748 (14.3%)
Russian	1,706 (14.0%)
Dutch	1,650 (13.6%)
Czech	1,001 (8.2%)

Table 4: Number of entities in Disease Ontology translated, number of Disease Ontology entities having at least one translation in Wikidata with first order links and the percentage of coverage.

The first line of Table 1 shows the matching between the English labels of the entities of Orphanet and Wikidata. $\mathcal{M}_{\mathrm{b}}\mathrm{l}$ and $\mathcal{M}_{\mathrm{M}}\mathrm{bl}$ are interesting here as they can be used as an indicator of a good match. A score of 1 means that one of the labels of Wikidata is the same as the preferred label from Orphanet ($\mathcal{M}_{\mathrm{b}}\mathrm{l}$) or one of the labels from Orphanet ($\mathcal{M}_{\mathrm{M}}\mathrm{bl}$). Considering that the scores are close to 1, the matching seems to be good.
In Table 1 we can see that Google Cloud Translation gives the best translations when evaluated with the Jaro Similarity. Nonetheless, there are still some small dissimilarities depending on the languages, it seems to works well for Spanish and less well for German and Polish. We can also note that for Portuguese, if the preferred label is well translated ($\mathcal{M}_{\mathrm{p}}\mathrm{l}$, $\mathcal{M}_{\mathrm{b}}\mathrm{l}$), it is less the case for the synonyms ($\mathcal{M}_{\mathrm{m}}\mathrm{bl}$).
Then, the first-order links from Wikidata have also some satisfactory results, there are also dissimilarities between the languages. Especially, first-order links seem to work better than the average in French. Compared to second-order links, first-order links are always better and the decrease in quality between both is substantial. Some noise is probably added by the intermediate ontologies.

4.3. Synonyms

Hailu et al. (2014) suggests that synonyms play an important role in translation. Therefore, in addition to high-quality translation, we are also interested in a high number of synonyms. In our case, the synonyms are the different labels available for each language for Orphanet and Wikidata, and the translations of the English labels for Google Cloud Translation. We want to evaluate the richness of each methods in terms of numbers of synonyms. For a fair comparison, for each language we only work on the subset where the entities in Wikidata have at least one label in the evaluated language.

Lang	Orphanet	Wiki 1st	Wiki 1+2nd	GCT
EN	2.3	5.8	166.77	2.3
FR	2.36	1.49	10.59	2.39
DE	2.56	1.84	5.93	2.65
ES	2.26	2.61	9.50	2.39
PL	2.54	2.01	6.88	2.65
IT	2.36	1.85	3.50	2.5
PT	1.62	1.60	2.40	2.41
NL	2.6	1.74	3.74	2.48
CS	2.2	1.74	1.71	2.13

Table 5: Average number of labels in the different sources in function of the language. For Orphanet we only use the subset of entities linked to entities in Wikidata with at least one label in the studied language. For Google Cloud Translation, it is the translation of the English labels of Orphanet.

Table 5 shows that generally Orphanet seems to have more synonyms than Wikidata when using first-order links only. And the fact GCT has more synonyms means that Orphanet has more labels in English than in other languages on the studied subset for majority language, except Dutch and Czech. Thus, this is not the case in English. For this language Wikidata is more diverse.

When using first and second-order links, the number of synonyms is much higher, especially for English. This is related to the fact that second-order links add many new relations. This new relations always have labels in English but not always habe labels in other languages.

5. Discussion

Regarding coverage, in terms of entities only, the coverage of first-order links is already high for Orphanet and Disease Ontology, respectively 84.9% and 97.2% (for English as, in our case, all the entities have English labels). The issue comes from the labels: even if Wikidata is multilingual, in our study we see that the information is mainly in English and French, but for the other studied languages the results are substantially worse. All the entities with a link have labels in English, more than half have labels in French and then for German, only around 20% of the 8,870 linked entities in Wikidata have at least one label in German. The languages we study are among the most used languages in Wikipedia. Thus, it is already an important amount of entities that could have their labels translated from English to another of these languages. As Wikidata is a collaborative project, this number should only increase over time. Second-order links help a lot for languages other than English.

Regarding quality, Google Cloud Translation is the best method. Compared to the results obtained by Silva et al. (2015) on the translation of a subpart of MeSH in Portuguese, the quality of the label translations seems to have greatly improved. Then translations obtained through first-order links are not so distant from Google Cloud Translation. However, the quality of the translations obtained through second-order links has a substantial difference with the translation coming from first-order links. Thus, we can expect Google Cloud Translation to have an advantage as Orphanet is primarily maintained in English and French and then translated by experts to other languages. Even if Google Cloud Translation is not free, translating the entirety of the English labels of Orphanet would only cost around 16$ with the pricing as of February 6, 2020.

For the synonyms, as Orphanet seems to have more labels in English than in the other languages, translating all the labels from English to the different languages allows having more synonyms than Orphanet in other languages. Moreover, Wikidata is poorer in terms of synonyms than Orphanet except for English. This is interesting as Google Cloud Translation seems to perform good translations, and having more synonyms in English also means that if we translate them with Google Cloud Translation we could have also more synonyms in other languages. It is also important to note that Google Cloud Translation only provides one translation by label. Second-order links also bring many more synonyms for all the languages, but especially for those which have a larger Wikidata.

6. Conclusions and Future Work

One of the limitations of this work concerns information that was not used. Especially in Orphanet and Wikidata, when an entity is linked to another ontology, there is additional information about the nature of the link, for example, whether it is an exact match or a more general entity. We did not use at all this information and it could be used to improve the links we create. Wikidata also contains more information about the entities than just the labels, e.g., Jiang et al. (2013) extracts multilingual textual definitions.

We also focus our study on one type of biomedical entities, diseases. The results of this work may not be generalized to all types of entities. Hailu et al. (2014) have found equivalent results for the translation of the Gene Ontology between English and German, but Silva et al. (2015) did not find the same results on their partial translation of MeSH.

Another limitation is our study about synonyms. Having the maximum number of synonyms is useful for entity recognition and normalization. Thus, here we only have quantitatively studied the synonyms, and have not explored their quality and diversity. First- and second-order link extraction from Wikidata seems to be a good method to have more synonyms. A further assessment with an expert that could validate the synonyms could be interesting.

Furthermore, as we are interested in entity recognition, a low coverage on the ontology is not correlated with a low coverage for entities in a corpus. In Bretschneider et al. (2014), by only translating a small sub-part of an ontology they could improve the coverage of the entities in their corpus by a high margin. It will be interesting to verify this on a dataset on disease recognition.

To summarize, as of now, Google Cloud Translate seems to be the best way to translate an ontology about diseases. If the ontology does not have many synonyms, Wikidata could be a way to expand language-wise the ontology. Wikidata also contains other information about its entities which could be interesting, but have not been used in this study such as symptoms and links to Wikipedia pages.

7. Bibliographical References

Alba, A., Coden, A., Gentile, A. L., Gruhl, D., Ristoski, P., and Welch, S. (2017). Multi-lingual Concept Extraction with Linked Data and Human-in-the-Loop. In *Proceedings of the Knowledge Capture Conference on - K-CAP 2017*, pages 1–8, Austin, TX, USA. ACM Press.

Andronis, C., Sharma, A., Virvilis, V., Deftereos, S., and Persidis, A. (2011). Literature mining, ontologies and information visualization for drug repurposing. *Briefings in Bioinformatics*, 12(4):357–368, 06.

Bretschneider, C., Oberkampf, H., Zillner, S., Bauer, B., and Hammon, M. (2014). Corpus-based Translation of Ontologies for Improved Multilingual Semantic Annotation. In *Proceedings of the Third Workshop on Semantic Web and Information Extraction*, pages 1–8, Dublin, Ireland. Association for Computational Linguistics and Dublin City University.

Hailu, N. D., Cohen, K. B., and Hunter, L. E. (2014). Ontology translation: A case study on translating the Gene Ontology from English to German. *Natural language processing and information systems : ... International Conference on Applications of Natural Language to Information Systems, NLDB ... revised papers. International Conference on Applications of Natural Language to Info.*, 8455:33–38, June.

INSERM. (1999a). Orphadata: Free access data from orphanet. `http://www.orphadata.org`. Accessed: 2020-02-11.

INSERM. (1999b). Orphanet: an online rare disease and orphan drug data base. `http://www.orpha.net`. Accessed: 2020-02-11.

Jaro, M. A. (1989). Advances in record-linkage methodology as applied to matching the 1985 census of tampa, florida. *Journal of the American Statistical Association*, 84(406):414–420.

Jiang, G. D., Solbrig, H. R., and Chute, C. G. (2013). A semantic web-based approach for harvesting multilingual textual definitions from wikipedia to support icd-11 revision. In *4th International Conference on Biomedical Ontology, ICBO 2013 Workshops on International Workshop on Vaccine and Drug Ontology Studies, VDOS 2013 and International Workshop on Definitions in Ontologies, DO 2013-Part of the Semantic Trilogy 2013*. CEUR-WS.

Langlotz, C. (2006). Radlex: a new method for indexing online educational materials. *Radiographics: a review publication of the Radiological Society of North America, Inc*, 26(6):1595.

Lehmann, J., Isele, R., Jakob, M., Jentzsch, A., Kontokostas, D., Mendes, P. N., Hellmann, S., Morsey, M., Van Kleef, P., Auer, S., et al. (2015). Dbpedia–a large-scale, multilingual knowledge base extracted from wikipedia. *Semantic Web*, 6(2):167–195.

Li, J., Zheng, S., Chen, B., Butte, A. J., Swamidass, S. J., and Lu, Z. (2015). A survey of current trends in computational drug repositioning. *Briefings in Bioinformatics*, 17(1):2–12, 03.

Maldonado, R., Goodwin, T. R., Skinner, M. A., and Harabagiu, S. M. (2017). Deep learning meets biomedical ontologies: knowledge embeddings for epilepsy. In *AMIA Annual Symposium Proceedings*, volume 2017, page 1233. American Medical Informatics Association.

Nayel, H. A. and Shashrekha, H. L. (2019). Integrating Dictionary Feature into A Deep Learning Model for Disease Named Entity Recognition. *arXiv:1911.01600 [cs]*, November. arXiv: 1911.01600.

Papineni, K., Roukos, S., Ward, T., and Zhu, W.-J. (2002). Bleu: a method for automatic evaluation of machine translation. In *Proceedings of the 40th annual meeting on association for computational linguistics*, pages 311–318. Association for Computational Linguistics.

Phan, N., Dou, D., Wang, H., Kil, D., and Piniewski, B. (2017). Ontology-based deep learning for human behavior prediction with explanations in health social networks. *Information sciences*, 384:298–313.

Schriml, L. M., Mitraka, E., Munro, J., Tauber, B., Schor, M., Nickle, L., Felix, V., Jeng, L., Bearer, C., Lichenstein, R., et al. (2019). Human disease ontology 2018 update: classification, content and workflow expansion. *Nucleic acids research*, 47(D1):D955–D962.

Silva, M. J., Chaves, T., and Simoes, B. (2015). An ontology-based approach for SNOMED CT translation. *ICBO 2015*.

Vrandečić, D. and Krötzsch, M. (2014). Wikidata: a free collaborative knowledgebase. *Communications of the ACM*, 57(10):78–85.

Proceedings of MultilingualBIO 2020, pages 29–32
Language Resources and Evaluation Conference (LREC 2020), Marseille, 11–16 May 2020

Transfer learning applied to text classification in Spanish radiological reports

Pilar López-Úbeda*, Manuel Carlos Díaz-Galiano*, L. Alfonso Ureña-López*, Maria-Teresa Martín-Valdivia*, Teodoro Martín-Noguerol†, Antonio Luna†
*Department of Computer Science, Advanced Studies Center in ICT (CEATIC)
Universidad de Jaén, Campus Las Lagunillas, 23071, Jaén, Spain
{plubeda, mcdiaz, laurena, maite}@ujaen.es
†MRI Unit, Radiology Department, HT médica. Carmelo Torres 2, 23007 Jaén, Spain
{t.martin.f, aluna70}@htime.org

Abstract

Pre-trained text encoders have rapidly advanced the state-of-the-art on many Natural Language Processing tasks. This paper presents the use of transfer learning methods applied to the automatic detection of codes in radiological reports in Spanish. Assigning codes to a clinical document is a popular task in NLP and in the biomedical domain. These codes can be of two types: standard classifications (e.g. ICD-10) or specific to each clinic or hospital. In this study we show a system using specific radiology clinic codes. The dataset is composed of 208,167 radiology reports labeled with 89 different codes. The corpus has been evaluated with three methods using the BERT model applied to Spanish: Multilingual BERT, BETO and XLM. The results are interesting obtaining 70% of F1-score with a pre-trained multilingual model.

Keywords: Transfer Learning, BERT Model, Spanish Radiological Reports, CT Scanning

1. Introduction

Radiology reports are text records taken by radiologists that detail the interpretation of a certain imaging modality exam including a description of radiological findings that could be the answer to a specific clinical question (patient's symptoms, clinical signs or specific syndromes). Structured text information in image reports can be applied in many scenarios, including clinical decision support (Demner-Fushman et al., 2009), detection of critical reports (Hripcsak et al., 2002), labeling of medical images (Dreyer et al., 2005; Hassanpour et al., 2017; Yadav et al., 2013), among other.

Natural language processing (NLP) has shown promise in automating the classification of free narrative text. In the NLP area this process is named Automatic Text Classification techniques (ATC). ATC is an automated process of assigning set of predefined categories to plain text documents (Witten and Frank, 2002).

The health care system employs a large number of categorization and classification systems to assist data management for a variety of tasks, including patient care, record storage and retrieval, statistical analysis, insurance and billing (Crammer et al., 2007; Scheurwegs et al., 2017; Wang et al., 2016). One of these classification systems is the International Classification of Diseases, Ten Version (ICD-10[1]). In 2017 a challenge was born at CLEF where the aim of the task was to automatically assign ICD-10 codes to the text content of death certificates in different languages such as English, French (Névéol et al., 2017), Hungarian, Italian (Névéol et al., 2018) or German (Dörendahl et al., 2019).

Regarding ATC, many techniques have been applied and studied. In traditional machine learning the most common algorithms known in the radiology community are: Naive Bayes, decision trees, logistic regression and SVM (Wang and Summers, 2012; Wei et al., 2005; Perotte et al., 2014). On the other hand, Recurrent Neural Networks (RNN) are used for sequence learning, where both input and output are word and label sequences, respectively. There are several studies related to RNN using Long Short-Term Memory (LSTM) (Tutubalina and Miftahutdinov, 2017) or CNN with an attention layer (Mullenbach et al., 2018). Finally, researchers have shown the value of transfer learning — pre-training a neural network model on a known task and then performing fine-tuning — using the trained neural network as the basis of a new purpose-specific model. BERT model is one of the best known models nowadays. BERT has also been used for multi-class classification with ICD-10 (Amin et al., 2019) obtaining good results with minimal effort.

This study is in the initial phase and it is focuses on automatic code assignment in Spanish, so it can also be an automatic multi-class classification task. The main contributions of this paper can be summarized as follows:

- We analyse the performance of the three transfer learning architectures using the BERT models in Spanish: Multilingual BERT, BETO and XLM.
- We achieve encouraging results for a collection of Spanish radiological reports.
- We also investigate the fine-tuning parameters for BERT, including pre-process of long text, layerwise learning rate, batch sizes and number of epochs.

2. Medical collection

Dataset is composed of 208,167 anonymized Computed Tomography (CT) examinations. This clinical corpus has been provided by the HT médica. Each report contains relevant information such as: reason for consultation, information regarding the hospital where the CT scan was conducted, type of scan (contrast or non-contrast), and location of the scan (body part).

Each radiology report requires a unique code from the 89 available codes. These labels are assigned according to

[1]https://icd.who.int/browse10/2016/en

the area where the scan was performed, the type of contrast (contrast or non-contrast) and other clinical indications such as fractures, trauma, inflammation, tumors, and so on. Figure 1 shows the most common codes in the dataset and the number of documents in which each label appears. We can see that the TX4, TC4 and TX5 codes are the ones that appear most frequently in the corpus.

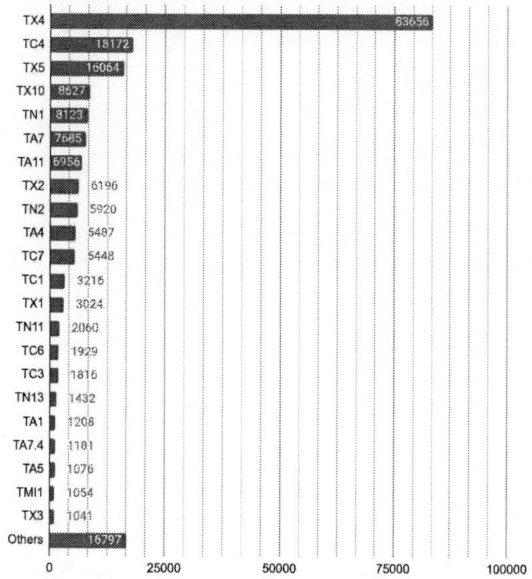

Figure 1: Most common labels and their frequency in the collection.

A weakness of the collection is that the text written by the specialists is in capital letters. Therefore, we pre-process the text by changing it to lower case.

Training, dev and test set The dataset was divided up to carry out the experimentation: 60% of the collection was used for the training set (124,899 documents), the development set was composed of 41,6434 documents (20%) and the remaining 20% for the test set (41,634 documents).
The sections of the CT examinations considered for this study were: the reason for the consultation, the location of the scan and the type of contrast used, avoiding hospital information because most of the examinations were done in the same hospital.

3. Code assignment methods

Transfer learning (Thrun, 1996) is an approach, by which a system can apply knowledge learned from previous tasks to a new task domain. This theory is inspired from the idea that people can intuitively use their previously learned experience to define and solve new problems.
For the automatic assignment of codes in Spanish, we have applied three transfer learning approaches based on BERT[2].
BERT (Bidirectional Encoder Representations from Transformers) (Devlin et al., 2018) is designed to pre-train deep bidirectional representations from unlabeled text by jointly conditioning on both left and right context in all layers. BERT uses a popular attention mechanism called transformer (Vaswani et al., 2017) that takes into account the context of words.
As a result, the pre-trained BERT model can be fine-tuned with just one additional output layer to create a multi-class classification model. This layer assigns a single code to a document.
In order to categorize radiology reports in Spanish, we have used three pre-trained models described below:

Multilingual (henceforth, M-BERT) follows the same model architecture and training procedure as BERT using data from Wikipedia in 104 languages (Pires et al., 2019). In M-BERT, the WordPiece modeling strategy allows the model to share embedding across languages.

BETO is a BERT model trained on a big Spanish corpus. BETO[3] is of size similar to a BERT for English and was trained with the Whole Word Masking technique (Cui et al., 2019).

XLM uses a pre-processing technique and a dual-language training mechanism with BERT in order to learn relations between words in different languages (Lample and Conneau, 2019). XLM presents a new training technique of BERT for multilingual classification tasks and the use of BERT as initialization of machine translation models.
In this study we show the performance of two XLM models: XLM trained with 17 languages (XLM-17) and trained with 100 languages (XLM-100)

4. Experiments and evaluation

4.1. Fine-tuning pre-trained parameters

In this step, we need to make decisions about the hyperparameters for the BERT model.
We use the BERT model with a hidden size of 768, 12 transformer blocks and 12 self-attention heads. For the optimizer, we leverage the *adam* optimizer which performs very well for NLP data and for BERT models in particular. For the purposes of fine-tuning, the authors recommend choosing from the following values: batch size, learning rate, max sequence and number of epoch. Table 4.1. illustrates the hyperparameters and their tested options, finally in each column we can see the model used and its selected parameter.

4.2. Results

In this section we present the results obtained by applying each BERT model. Since the corpus of radiological reports is in Spanish, we have applied the available models for this language in transfer learning.
The metrics used to carry out the experiments are the measures popularly known in the NLP community, namely macro-precision, macro-recall and macro-averaged F1-score.
Table 2 shows the results achieved and we can see that the results are encouraging, having a large list of codes to assign. XLM gets the best results by upgrading to BETO and

[2]https://github.com/google-research/bert

[3]https://github.com/dccuchile/beto

Parameter	Options	M-BERT	BETO	XLM-100	XLM-17
Batch size	[16, 32, 64]	32	16	16	16
Max sequence	[256, 512]	256	256	256	256
Learning rate	[2e-5, 3e-5]	3e-5	2e-5	2e-5	2e-5
Epoch	[3, 4, 5]	4	5	5	5

Table 1: Hyperparameters tested and options chosen in each model.

Pre-trainined Model	Precision	Recall	F1-score
M-BERT	65.41	62.07	62.33
BETO	69.86	65.34	66.34
XLM-100	**75.05**	69.10	70.64
XML-17	74.83	**69.79**	**70.84**

Table 2: Results obtained for code assignment in radiological reports.

M-BERT. XLM mixes several languages but it is enough to learn in the radiology reports and to detect the correct code. XLM-100 obtains the best precision (75%) and XLM-17 the best recall (69.7%). The best F1-score was also obtained with XLM-17 getting 70%.
Performing a brief analysis of the mislabeled codes, we found that the 23 worst-labeled codes had 2,443 documents to be trained, which is 1.96% of the total training set. In addition, the average number of training documents is 106, so they do not have enough information to learn. According to the evaluation of each code, Figure 2 shows the number of codes and their result ranges using the F1 score.

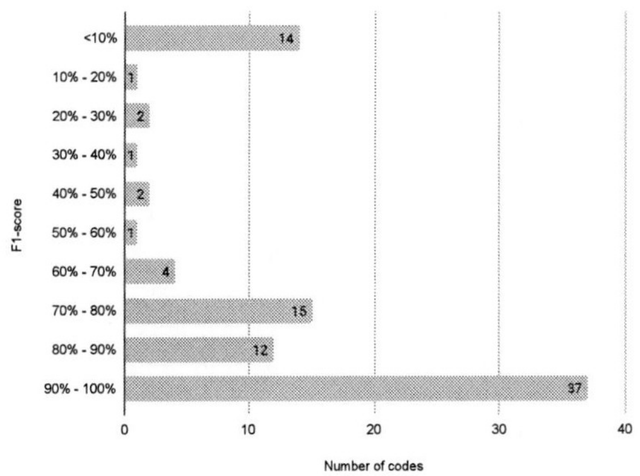

Figure 2: Results obtained in the F1-score and number of codes evaluated.

5. Limitations and future work

Our project is in a beginner's state and has limitations that need to be improved in the future. The limitations we found are shown below:

- Occasionally, the texts of the radiological reports are longer than allowed in the BERT model (max sequence of 512).
- The texts provided by the specialists are in capital letters, we pre-process the text by changing it to lower case.
- There are codes with few examples for training, so the system fails to classify.

We plan to make future improvements to the automatic classification system. These improvements can be summarized in the following points:

- We will perform a deep error analysis and see the behavior of each model applied to our corpus.
- We will analyze why XLM has achieved better results than BETO, being XLM trained for different languages.
- Strategies with embeddings to obtain the representation vector of each word will be used in future work.
- We will make changes to the model, for example, adding new layers or concatenating new features extracted from the corpus.
- We will improve BERT's vocabulary to find more words related to the biomedical domain. BioBERT (Lee et al., 2019) currently exists for English, we could make an adaptation or create a similar model with Spanish.
- There are parts of the text that are more important than others, for example the location of the exploration, in the future we plan to detect these features so that the model learns better.

6. Conclusion

In this study we conducted a multi-class task to detect codes in radiology reports written in Spanish. We have carried out experiments that are the state-of-the-art pre-training for NLP: BERT model. We apply different approaches using this model such as Multilingual BERT, BETO and XLM.
Recent advances in transfer learning model have opened another way to extract features and classify medical documents. We have a collection of over 200,000 CT scans and each text can have 89 possible codes. Each code is associated with the document for a reason. The most important reasons include: location of the body where the CT scan was performed or a previous finding or disease.
Using the XLM algorithm trained with 17 different languages we obtain a 70% of F1-score, detecting that the worst predictions are those codes that have scarce examples to train.

This study is at an early stage so we have described limitations and future work to further improve the code assignment task.

7. Acknowledgements

This work has been partially supported by the Fondo Europeo de Desarrollo Regional (FEDER), LIVING-LANG project (RTI2018-094653-B-C21), under the Spanish Government.

8. Bibliographical References

Amin, S., Neumann, G., Dunfield, K., Vechkaeva, A., Chapman, K. A., and Wixted, M. K. (2019). Mlt-dfki at clef ehealth 2019: Multi-label classification of icd-10 codes with bert. *CLEF (Working Notes)*.

Crammer, K., Dredze, M., Ganchev, K., Talukdar, P., and Carroll, S. (2007). Automatic code assignment to medical text. In *Biological, translational, and clinical language processing*, pages 129–136.

Cui, Y., Che, W., Liu, T., Qin, B., Yang, Z., Wang, S., and Hu, G. (2019). Pre-training with whole word masking for chinese bert. *arXiv preprint arXiv:1906.08101*.

Demner-Fushman, D., Chapman, W. W., and McDonald, C. J. (2009). What can natural language processing do for clinical decision support? *Journal of biomedical informatics*, 42(5):760–772.

Devlin, J., Chang, M.-W., Lee, K., and Toutanova, K. (2018). Bert: Pre-training of deep bidirectional transformers for language understanding. *arXiv preprint arXiv:1810.04805*.

Dörendahl, A., Leich, N., Hummel, B., Schönfelder, G., and Grune, B. (2019). Overview of the clef ehealth 2019 multilingual information extraction. In *Working Notes of CLEF 2019 - Conference and Labs of the Evaluation Forum*.

Dreyer, K. J., Kalra, M. K., Maher, M. M., Hurier, A. M., Asfaw, B. A., Schultz, T., Halpern, E. F., and Thrall, J. H. (2005). Application of recently developed computer algorithm for automatic classification of unstructured radiology reports: validation study. *Radiology*, 234(2):323–329.

Hassanpour, S., Langlotz, C. P., Amrhein, T. J., Befera, N. T., and Lungren, M. P. (2017). Performance of a machine learning classifier of knee mri reports in two large academic radiology practices: a tool to estimate diagnostic yield. *American Journal of Roentgenology*, 208(4):750–753.

Hripcsak, G., Austin, J. H., Alderson, P. O., and Friedman, C. (2002). Use of natural language processing to translate clinical information from a database of 889,921 chest radiographic reports. *Radiology*, 224(1):157–163.

Lample, G. and Conneau, A. (2019). Cross-lingual language model pretraining. *arXiv preprint arXiv:1901.07291*.

Lee, J., Yoon, W., Kim, S., Kim, D., Kim, S., So, C. H., and Kang, J. (2019). Biobert: pre-trained biomedical language representation model for biomedical text mining. *arXiv preprint arXiv:1901.08746*.

Mullenbach, J., Wiegreffe, S., Duke, J., Sun, J., and Eisenstein, J. (2018). Explainable prediction of medical codes from clinical text. *arXiv preprint arXiv:1802.05695*.

Névéol, A., Robert, A., Anderson, R., Cohen, K. B., Grouin, C., Lavergne, T., Rey, G., Rondet, C., and Zweigenbaum, P. (2017). Clef ehealth 2017 multilingual information extraction task overview: Icd10 coding of death certificates in english and french. In *CLEF (Working Notes)*.

Névéol, A., Robert, A., Grippo, F., Morgand, C., Orsi, C., Pelikan, L., Ramadier, L., Rey, G., and Zweigenbaum, P. (2018). Clef ehealth 2018 multilingual information extraction task overview: Icd10 coding of death certificates in french, hungarian and italian. In *CLEF (Working Notes)*.

Perotte, A., Pivovarov, R., Natarajan, K., Weiskopf, N., Wood, F., and Elhadad, N. (2014). Diagnosis code assignment: models and evaluation metrics. *Journal of the American Medical Informatics Association*, 21(2):231–237.

Pires, T., Schlinger, E., and Garrette, D. (2019). How multilingual is multilingual bert? *arXiv preprint arXiv:1906.01502*.

Scheurwegs, E., Cule, B., Luyckx, K., Luyten, L., and Daelemans, W. (2017). Selecting relevant features from the electronic health record for clinical code prediction. *Journal of biomedical informatics*, 74:92–103.

Thrun, S. (1996). Is learning the n-th thing any easier than learning the first? In *Advances in neural information processing systems*, pages 640–646.

Tutubalina, E. and Miftahutdinov, Z. (2017). An encoder-decoder model for icd-10 coding of death certificates. *arXiv preprint arXiv:1712.01213*.

Vaswani, A., Shazeer, N., Parmar, N., Uszkoreit, J., Jones, L., Gomez, A. N., Kaiser, Ł., and Polosukhin, I. (2017). Attention is all you need. In *Advances in neural information processing systems*, pages 5998–6008.

Wang, S. and Summers, R. M. (2012). Machine learning and radiology. *Medical image analysis*, 16(5):933–951.

Wang, S., Chang, X., Li, X., Long, G., Yao, L., and Sheng, Q. Z. (2016). Diagnosis code assignment using sparsity-based disease correlation embedding. *IEEE Transactions on Knowledge and Data Engineering*, 28(12):3191–3202.

Wei, L., Yang, Y., Nishikawa, R. M., and Jiang, Y. (2005). A study on several machine-learning methods for classification of malignant and benign clustered microcalcifications. *IEEE transactions on medical imaging*, 24(3):371–380.

Witten, I. H. and Frank, E. (2002). Data mining: practical machine learning tools and techniques with java implementations. *Acm Sigmod Record*, 31(1):76–77.

Yadav, K., Sarioglu, E., Smith, M., and Choi, H.-A. (2013). Automated outcome classification of emergency department computed tomography imaging reports. *Academic Emergency Medicine*, 20(8):848–854.

Proceedings of MultilingualBIO 2020, pages 33–36
Language Resources and Evaluation Conference (LREC 2020), Marseille, 11–16 May 2020

Automated Processing of Multilingual Online News for the Monitoring of Animal Infectious Diseases

Sarah Valentin[1,2,*], Renaud Lancelot[1], Mathieu Roche[2]
[1] UMR ASTRE, CIRAD, F-34398 Montpellier, France.
ASTRE, Univ Montpellier, CIRAD, INRAE, Montpellier, France.
[2] UMR TETIS, CIRAD, F-34398 Montpellier, France.
TETIS, Univ Montpellier, AgroParisTech, CIRAD, CNRS, INRAE, Montpellier, France.
[*] Corresponding author: sarah.valentin@cirad.fr

Abstract

The Platform for Automated extraction of animal Disease Information from the web (PADI-web) is an automated system which monitors the web for detecting and identifying emerging animal infectious diseases. The tool automatically collects news via customised multilingual queries, classifies them and extracts epidemiological information. We detail the processing of multilingual online sources by PADI-web and analyse the translated outputs in a case study.

Keywords: Animal health, Web monitoring, Text mining, Multilingual

1. Introduction

The timely detection of (re)emerging animal infectious diseases worldwide is a keystone for risk assessment and risk management regarding both human and animal health. Traditional surveillance relies on official notifications from intergovernmental organisations such as the World Organisation for Animal Health (OIE) and the Food and Agriculture Organization of the United Nations (FAO). While these systems provide verified and structured information, they are prone to notification delays and are not appropriate to detect new threats. To enhance early detection performances, surveillance activities increasingly integrate unstructured data from informal sources such as online news (Bahk et al., 2015). The daily curation and analysis of web-based information are time-consuming. Thus, several systems were designed to automatize the monitoring of online sources regarding a wide range of health threats, such as MedISys (Mantero et al., 2011), HealthMap (Freifeld et al., 2008), GPHIN (Blench, 2008), ProMED (Madoff, 2004) or PADI-web (Valentin et al., 2020). PADI-web[1] (Platform for Automated extraction of Disease Information from the web) is an automated system dedicated to the monitoring of online news sources for the detection of animal health infectious diseases. PADI-web was developed to suit the need of the French Epidemic Intelligence System (FEIS, or Veille sanitaire internationale in French), which is part of the animal health epidemiological surveillance Platform (ESA Platform). The tool automatically collects news with customised multilingual queries, classifies them and extracts epidemiological information. In this paper, we describe how the PADI-web pipeline processes multilingual textual data. We also provide a case study to highlight the added-value of integrating multiple languages for web-based surveillance.

2. Multilingual news processing

PADI-web pipeline includes four consecutive steps (Figure 1), extensively detailed elsewhere (Valentin et al., 2020): data collection, data processing, data classification and information extraction.

2.1. Data collection

PADI-web collects news articles from Google News on a daily basis, through two types of customised really simple syndication (RSS) feeds (Arsevska et al., 2016). Disease-based feeds target specific monitored diseases, thus they contain disease terms such as *avian flu* or *African swine fever*. To be able to detect emerging threats or undiagnosed diseases, PADI-web also relies on symptom-based RSS feeds. These feeds consist of combinations of symptoms and species (hosts), for instance, *abortions AND cows*. To retrieve non-English sources, we also implemented non-English feeds by translating existing ones in other languages. The languages were selected to target risk areas regarding specific diseases (e.g. we integrated RSS feeds in Arabic for monitoring foot-and-mouth disease in endemic countries). To translate the disease terms, we used Agrovoc[2], a controlled vocabulary developed by the Food and Agriculture Organization (FAO).

2.2. Data processing

PADI-web fetches all the news webpages retrieved by the RSS feeds. The title and text of each news article are cleaned to remove irrelevant elements (pictures, ads, hyperlinks, etc.). The language of the source is detected using the *langdetect* python library. All non-English news articles are translated into English using the Translator API of the Microsoft Azure system [3].

2.3. Data classification

To select the relevant news (i.e. the news describing a current outbreak as well as prevention and control measures,

[1] https://padi-web.cirad.fr/en/

[2] http://aims.fao.org/vest-registry/vocabularies/agrovoc

[3] https://azure.microsoft.com/en-gb/services/cognitive-services/translator-text-api/

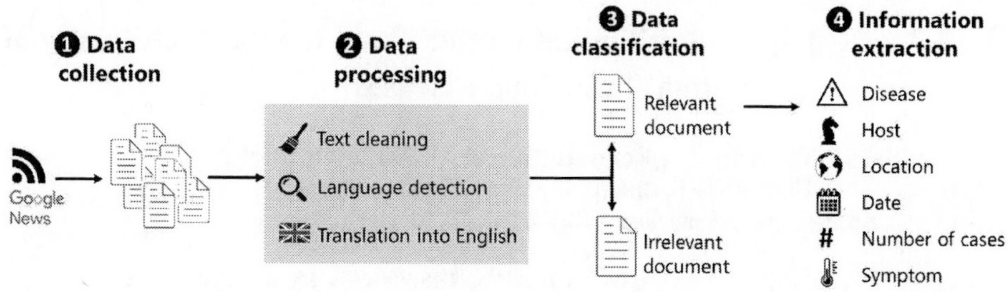

Figure 1: PADI-web pipeline

preparedness, socioeconomic impacts, etc.), PADI-web relies on an automated classifier developed with a supervised machine learning approach. The training dataset consists in a corpus of 600 annotated pieces of news labelled by an epidemiology expert (200 relevant news articles and 400 irrelevant news articles). Using the scikitlearn python library, several models from different families are trained:

- Linear classifiers: Logistic Regression, Gaussian and Multinomial Naive Bayes
- Support vector machines: Linear Support Vector Machine (Linear SVM)
- Decision tree: Random Forest
- Quadratic classifiers: Quadratic Discriminant Analysis
- Instance-based learning models: K-nearest neighbor learner
- Neural networks: Multilayer Perceptron

The model obtaining the highest mean accuracy score along the 5-fold cross-validation scheme is subsequently used to classify each new retrieved article. Currently, Random Forest (composed of 50 trees with a maximum depth of 12) and the Multilayer Perceptron are the best classifiers, obtaining an average accuracy score of 0.944 ± 0.01 (Table 1).

Classifier	Average accuracy score	Standard deviation
Multilayer Perceptron	**0.944**	0.01
Random Forest	**0.944**	0.01
Linear SVM	0.935	0.02
Quadratic Discriminant Analysis	0.905	0.01
Gaussian Naive Bayes	0.896	0.01
K-nearest neighbor learner, K=2	0.896	0.04
Logistic Regression	0.881	0.04
Multinomial Naive Bayes	0.867	0.04

Table 1: Results of the relevance classification in terms of average accuracy score, for different classifiers.

2.4. Information extraction

The extraction of epidemiological information relies on a combined method founded on rule-based systems and data mining techniques (Arsevska et al., 2018). Diseases, hosts and symptoms are extracted using a list of terms of disease names, hosts and clinical signs. To obtain our list of terms, we use BioTex (Lossio-Ventura et al., 2014), a tool for automatic extraction of biomedical terms from free text, as detailed elsewhere (Arsevska et al., 2016). Locations are identified by matching the text with location names from the GeoNames gazetteer (Ahlers, 2013) and dates with the rule-based HeidelTime system (Strotgen and Gertz, 2010). The number of cases is extracted from a list of regular expressions matching numbers in numerical or textual form. A confidence index is automatically assigned to the extracted entities to reflect the probability that they correspond to the desired piece of epidemiological information.

The models for classification (Section 2.3.) and information extraction (Section 2.4.) tasks have been learnt with labeled data in English. English is a "bridge-language" (or "pivot language") for PADI-web. In this context, a translation method has been applied for non-English news before using the classification and information extraction algorithms of the PADI-web pipeline.

3. Case study

We conducted a preliminary case study to evaluate the processing of non-English sources by PADI-web.

3.1. Methods

We extracted the translated news articles from PADI-web database from 01 July 2019 to 31 July 2019 (1 month period). We manually reviewed each news to select the ones containing an animal disease event. An event corresponds to the occurrence of a disease at a specific location and date. Then, we compared the detected events with official events extracted from the FAO Emergency Prevention System for Priority Animal and Plant Pests and Disease (EMPRES-i)[4]. This system receives information from different official data sources, such as governments or OIE, and is a global reference database for animal diseases. We calculated the delay between the official notification and the detection by PADI-web (corresponding to the publication date of the news article). The events present in online news but absent from the official database are considered as unofficial (they cannot be verified). For both official and unofficial events detected by non-English sources, we deter-

[4] http://empres-i.fao.org/eipws3g/.

Disease	Country (no of events)	Source language[a]	Detected in English news	Range of detection delays (days)[b]
African swine fever	Bulgaria (n=1)	TR, IT	yes	-10
	China (n=6)	FR, KO, ZH-CN	yes	- 12 to 1
	Laos (n=1)	ZH-CN	no	5
	Slovakia (n=1)	DE, IT, ZH-CN	yes	0
Avian influenza	Denmark (n=1)	KO	no	4
	Mexico (n=1)	KO	no	1
	Taiwan (n=2)	KO	no	-12 to -2
Foot-and-mouth disease	Morocco (n=1)	AR, FR	no	-5 to 0

Table 2: Official events detected by non-English sources.
[a]Languages: AR: Arabic, DE: German, FR: French, IT: Italian, KO: Korean, TR: Turkish, ZH-CN: Chinese.
[b] Lag between the official notification and the detection by PADI-web.

mined if they were also detected by English news retrieved by PADI-web during the same period.

3.2. Results and discussion

From 01 July 2019 to 31 July 2019, PADI-web retrieved 104 online news, among which 47 online news contained one or several animal disease events. The remaining 57 news were related to control measures (n=34), outbreak follow-up (n=6), human disease outbreak (n=7), disease awareness (n=2), or were irrelevant (n=8). The low number of irrelevant news (8/104) indicates that the classification module was able to perform well on translated news.
The information extraction module extracted 93 disease entities, 218 host entities, 47 dates, 584 locations, 125 symptoms and 45 numbers of cases. PADI-web detected 14 distinct official events from 35 non-English online news (Table 2), involving 3 diseases and 8 countries. English-news did not detect six out of 14 events. The events were detected up to 12 days before their official notification. Besides, PADI-web discovered 5 unofficial events from 12 non-English online news (Table 3.), among which 4 were not detected by English-news.

Disease	Country (no of events)	Source (language[a])	Detected in English news
Anthrax	Guinea (n=1)	FR	no
Eastern equine encephalitis	USA (n=1)	IT	yes
Foot-and-mouth disease	Morocco (n=1)	AR, FR	no
Lumpy skin disease	Kazakhstan (n=1)	RU	no
Peste des petits ruminants	Algeria (n=1)	FR	no

Table 3: Unofficial events detected by non-English sources.
[a]Languages: AR: Arabic, FR: French, IT: Italian, RU: Russian.

During one-month, the non-English sources increased both the sensitivity and the timeliness of PADI-web in detecting official events. This is consistent with the fact that local sources are more reactive in reporting outbreaks from their area or country. The added value of integrating multilingual sources was also highlighted by an in-depth comparison of event-based tools in the human health domain (Barboza et al., 2014).

During the manual analysis, we found out that two diseases were wrongly translated. The most frequent errors occurred when translating *African swine fever* from several languages. We found the following wrong expressions: *African swine plague*, *African pig plague*, *plague of pig*, *African wild boar plague*. In one piece of Chinese news, the translated form was *swine fever in Africa*, which led to the detection of a false location (*Africa*). Errors also occurred in its acronyms translation (*ASP* instead of *ASF*). From Russian news, lumpy skin disease was translated as *nodular dermatitis*. Many animal disease names consist in a combination of host, symptom and location terms. Thus, they are prone to translation errors which should be taken into account to avoid impacting the performances of monitoring tools. Translated texts underline the limits of relying on vocabulary matching for entity recognition. Existing NER models based on machine learning do not include domain-specific entities such as diseases and hosts. However, the python package spaCy allows adding new classes to the default entities, by training its existing model with new labelled examples. Such an approach could enhance the detection of out of vocabulary terms produced by translation.

4. Conclusion

We described how we integrated multilingual sources in the existing PADI-web system. The preliminary evaluation yielded promising results regarding the added-value of integrating non-English news to web-based surveillance. In future work, we will conduct a more in-depth analysis of the translated outputs in terms of sensitivity and timeliness, and we will evaluate the quality of the geographical entities after applying the translation task. Besides, we aim to improve the detection of named entities such as disease names by training NER models.

5. Acknowledgements

This work was funded by the French General Directorate for Food (DGAL), the French Agricultural Research Centre for International Development (CIRAD), the SONGES Project (FEDER and Occitanie) and the MOOD project. This work was supported by the French National Research

Agency (ANR) under the Investments for the Future Program (ANR-16-CONV-0004). This work has received funding from the European Union's Horizon 2020 research and innovation programme under Grant Agreement MOOD 874850. The authors thank J. Rabatel, E. Arsevska, S. Falala and the members of the French Epidemic Intelligence in Animal Health (A. Mercier, J. Cauchard and C. Dupuy) for their contribution and expertise in developing PADI-web.

6. Bibliographical References

Ahlers, D. (2013). Assessment of the Accuracy of GeoNames Gazetteer Data. In *Proceedings of the 7th Workshop on Geographic Information Retrieval*, pages 74–81, New York, NY, USA. ACM.

Arsevska, E., Roche, M., Hendrikx, P., Chavernac, D., Falala, S., Lancelot, R., and Dufour, B. (2016). Identification of terms for detecting early signals of emerging infectious disease outbreaks on the web. *Computers and Electronics in Agriculture*, 123:104–115.

Arsevska, E., Valentin, S., Rabatel, J., de Goër de Hervé, J., Falala, S., Lancelot, R., and Roche, M. (2018). Web monitoring of emerging animal infectious diseases integrated in the French Animal Health Epidemic Intelligence System. *PLOS ONE*, 13(8):e0199960, August.

Bahk, C. Y., Scales, D. A., Mekaru, S. R., Brownstein, J. S., and Freifeld, C. C. (2015). Comparing timeliness, content, and disease severity of formal and informal source outbreak reporting. *BMC Infectious Diseases*, 15(1), December.

Barboza, P., Vaillant, L., Le Strat, Y., Hartley, D. M., Nelson, N. P., Mawudeku, A., Madoff, L. C., Linge, J. P., Collier, N., Brownstein, J. S., and Astagneau, P. (2014). Factors influencing performance of internet-based biosurveillance systems used in epidemic intelligence for early detection of infectious diseases outbreaks. *PLoS ONE*, 9(3):e90536, March.

Blench, M. (2008). Global public health intelligence network (GPHIN). In *8th Conference of the Association for Machine Translation in the Americas*, pages 8–12.

Freifeld, C. C., Mandl, K. D., Reis, B. Y., and Brownstein, J. S. (2008). HealthMap: Global Infectious Disease Monitoring through Automated Classification and Visualization of Internet Media Reports. *Journal of the American Medical Informatics Association*, 15(2):150–157, March.

Lossio-Ventura, J. A., Jonquet, C., Roche, M., and Teisseire, M. (2014). BIOTEX: A system for Biomedical Terminology Extraction, Ranking, and Validation. In *International Semantic Web Conference*.

Madoff, L. C. (2004). ProMED-mail: an early warning system for emerging diseases. *Clinical infectious diseases*, 39(2):227–232.

Mantero, J., Belyaeva, J., Linge, J., European Commission, Joint Research Centre, and Institute for the Protection and the Security of the Citizen. (2011). *How to maximise event-based surveillance web-systems: the example of ECDC/JRC collaboration to improve the performance of MedISys.* Publications Office, Luxembourg. OCLC: 870614547.

Strotgen, J. and Gertz, M. (2010). HeidelTime: High Quality Rule-Based Extraction and Normalization of Temporal Expressions. In *Proceedings of the 5th International Workshop on Semantic Evaluation*, pages 321–324, July.

Valentin, S., Arsevska, E., Falala, S., de Goër, J., Lancelot, R., Mercier, A., Rabatel, J., and Roche, M. (2020). PADI-web: A multilingual event-based surveillance system for monitoring animal infectious diseases. *Computers and Electronics in Agriculture*, 169:105163, February.

Association for Computational Linguistics
209 N. Eighth Street
Stroudsburg, Pennsylvania 18360

ISBN 978-1-7138-1270-8

CURRAN ASSOCIATES INC.
proceedings.com